DISCOVER
BOURNEMOUTH

AND THE MAIN PLACES OF INTEREST IN CHRISTCHURCH AND RINGWOOD

RODNEY COOPER

HALSGROVE

First published in Great Britain in 2010

British Library Cataloguing-in-Publication Data
A CIP record for this title is available from the British Library

ISBN 978 0 85704 067 1

HALSGROVE
Halsgrove House,
Ryelands Industrial Estate,
Bagley Road, Wellington, Somerset TA21 9PZ
Tel: 01823 653777   Fax: 01823 216796
email: sales@halsgrove.com

Part of the Halsgrove group of companies
Information on all Halsgrove titles is available at: www.halsgrove.com

Printed and bound in Italy by Grafiche Flaminia

CONTENTS

INTRODUCTION

Bournemouth is an excellent holiday location and a good base from which to explore the surrounding area. The town itself has a wonderful safe sandy beach, beautiful gardens, tree lined roads and a varied night life which caters for all ages. There are many hotels, cafés and restaurants.

The town, with its Victorian heritage, is blessed with several beautiful churches and grand buildings, many of which have an interesting history and are well worth a visit. This guide takes you around the heart of Bournemouth with notes on points of interest and then to several locations towards the outskirts of the town which are of particular, mainly historical, interest.

Within easy reach of Bournemouth are many places of exceptional natural beauty and with a history reaching back to early times.

Those included in the guide are places which make for an interesting, leisurely, pleasant and inexpensive day out, although you may find that you require more than a single visit to see all the attractions in that region.

Within each area, the attractions are grouped by location, so the closest to the one you are reading are usually the ones on the preceding and following pages. Postcodes are given for people with satellite navigation systems. In many cases directions are given from the location on the previous page.

Telephone numbers are shown and you are strongly advised to confirm opening hours when you plan your visit. In particular you might find that an attraction is open during a particular weekend, public holiday or school holiday, even though the dates fall outside those given in this guide. Where places are shown in **bold italics** then there is a main mention of it elsewhere in the guide.

It is recommended that one of the first things to be done on arrival in Bournemouth is a visit the Tourist Information Centre in ***Westover Road*** and purchase for a nominal fee a copy of the current 'What's On' which gives details of events and performances in the Borough during the month.

Acknowledgements

I would like to thank everyone who has contributed to this book, some of whom I have mentioned, in particular to Linda Barker who introduced me to the delights of the Wimborne Road Cemetery, Michael Hodges who corrected my factual errors on Christchurch and shared a happy lunch and pint with me and Dave Kelsey who showed me the night spots of Bournemouth. But above all to my wife, Elaine, who navigated our way to the various locations, knocked my scribbles into readable text and gave gentle criticism and support when necessary. Without her continuous support, little of what I have achieved in life would have been possible.

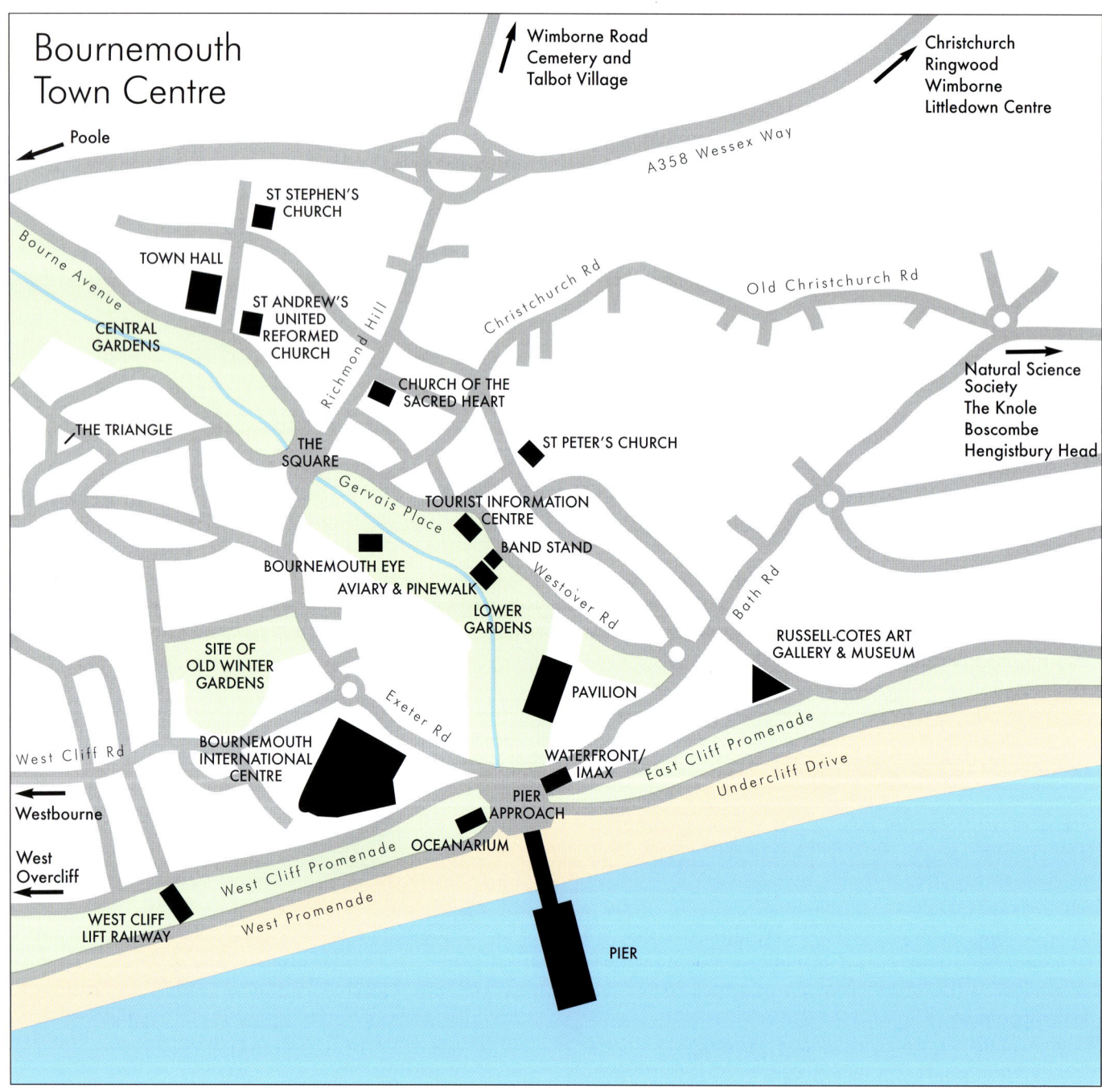

Bournemouth Town Centre

Poole

Wimborne Road
Cemetery and
Talbot Village

Christchurch
Ringwood
Wimborne
Littledown Centre

A358 Wessex Way

ST STEPHEN'S
CHURCH

TOWN HALL

Bourne Avenue

CENTRAL
GARDENS

ST ANDREW'S
UNITED
REFORMED
CHURCH

Christchurch Rd

Old Christchurch Rd

Richmond Hill

CHURCH OF THE
SACRED HEART

Natural Science
Society
The Knole
Boscombe
Hengistbury Head

THE TRIANGLE

THE
SQUARE

ST PETER'S CHURCH

Gervais Place

TOURIST INFORMATION
CENTRE

BAND STAND

BOURNEMOUTH EYE

AVIARY & PINEWALK

LOWER
GARDENS

Westover Rd

Bath Rd

RUSSELL-COTES ART
GALLERY & MUSEUM

SITE OF
OLD WINTER
GARDENS

PAVILION

Exeter Rd

East Cliff Promenade

West Cliff Rd

BOURNEMOUTH
INTERNATIONAL
CENTRE

WATERFRONT/
IMAX

Undercliff Drive

Westbourne

West
Overcliff

PIER
APPROACH

OCEANARIUM

West Cliff Promenade

West Promenade

WEST CLIFF
LIFT RAILWAY

PIER

BOURNEMOUTH

Although a 1575 map in the British Museum refers to 'Bourne Mouth in the County of Dorset', most historians take the birth of Bournemouth as 1810 when Lewis Tregonwell purchased a plot of land on which to build his seaside villa. This piece of land is now the site of the Royal Exeter Hotel. Whilst on holiday Tregonwell had taken a day trip from Mudeford to the mouth of the Bourne River and had instantly fallen in love with the area. From that time he lived mainly in Bournemouth but when he

died in 1832 at the age of 73 he was buried in his home village of Anderson. However in 1846, his wife had his remains moved to a vault in **St Peter's Church**. Whilst living in Bournemouth he began planting pine trees on the steep valley (or Chine) leading down to the beach, as it was believed that breathing the fragrance

from these trees was beneficial to one's health. Many landowners did the same and Bournemouth became known as the 'pine city by the sea'. Many of these pines can still be seen in Bournemouth's chines to this day. There are several areas around Bournemouth that have a much longer history. In particular it is believed that **Hengistbury Head** was where the first town in Britain was located. Bournemouth was granted Borough status by Queen Victoria in 1890.

Bournemouth is arguably Britain's premier resort. It is renowned for its seven miles of golden beaches – you can walk along the promenade from **Hengistbury Head** in the east to Poole in the west. It is also known for its gardens and 25% of the borough is green space, more than any other town in the South of England, a point which is fully appreciated only when viewed from above, for example from the Bournemouth Eye. Each of its ten parks, has its own Green Flag Award. There are several chines and the description of Bournemouth as the 'place where the gardens meet the sea' is certainly appropriate.

Bournemouth is often regarded as a retirement location and whereas it is true that many people do retire to the town, a few years

ago Bournemouth had the highest number of start-up companies in the country and ranked fifth in a survey as the most popular destination to which people relocate. Several financial companies have their UK head offices here. It has a strong student presence and is the largest provider of international education through its language

schools outside of London. This gives the town a young feel. Besides the wonderful beach and gardens, it has a lively, bustling town centre, both during the day and well into the night. Most of the town's excellent **sporting facilities** are available to tourists. Its hotels have been voted the best value hotels in the world and many have recently been refurbished. Besides there being plenty to do and see in Bournemouth, it is also a perfect base for trips to the historic towns of **Christchurch** and **Ringwood** which is also the gateway to the New Forest. The historic towns of Poole, Wareham and Wimborne are within easy reach, as is the Isle of Purbeck (Britain's only natural World Heritage site*)*; all of these are covered in the author's forthcoming companion book – *Discover Poole*. Then after a day of site-seeing, visitors can return to Bournemouth to enjoy the Borough's excellent night life.

BOURNEMOUTH PIER

Piers date from the time when journeys to distant parts of the country had to be undertaken by a rather uncomfortable stage coach. A more comfortable way, if you could afford it, was to go by boat but then there was the problem of alighting on arrival. This often meant walking to the beach from the ship through the none too warm sea. So landing stages were built, which later developed into piers for pleasure use when it was realised people enjoyed walking above the water. Bournemouth initially had a landing jetty on wheels, which was replaced by a permanent jetty in 1856. Work on building a permanent pier started in 1859 but a few weeks later everything was washed away by a violent storm. Then the bank holding the funds went broke. Eventually, in 1861, Bournemouth

The 850-seat Pier Theatre opened for the first time in 1959 and now, after fires at other similar theatres in the country, it is one of only six pier-theatres remaining. Tel: 01202 306126 for bookings.

The Key West Bar at the end of the pier was refurbished in 2007. Here you can have a drink or a meal. Tel: 01202 306155 for reservations.

had its first (wooden) pier, with a large T piece at the end to act as a shelter for steamers. Unfortunately ship worm ate into the wooden piles and they had to be replaced with cast iron piles five years later. The following year a storm removed the T piece and a later storm blew away part of the main pier. A new, iron pier opened in 1880. Several changes were made over the years, in particular the widening of the landing stages. In July 1940 a 120 feet section in the centre of the pier was demolished under the threat of invasion from German forces; it was rebuilt between 1946 and 1950. During the winter of 2007 refurbishment work was carried out on the pier to update it for current use.

In the summer the Pier Theatre holds children's shows during the day and there is a small fun fair at the end of the pier. Fishing permits can be obtained from the sea front Tourist Information Centre to the east of the pier. There is normally a small entrance charge to the pier during the peak seasons but entrance is free at other times or if going to the Pier Theatre. The pier's opening times are flexible depending on the time of the year and events on the pier but are normally from 0900 – 1630 in the winter and 0900 – 1800 in the summer.

There is a variety of boat rides and cruises that can be taken from

Shockwave is a 500HP jet boat that leaves every 15 minutes and gives 10 minutes of an exhilarating, high speed ride round the bay.

There is a regular ferry service to Brownsea Island from Easter to the end of September departing every 90 minutes and taking 30 minutes. Other cruises go Round the Bay (30mins), to Sandbanks & Poole (1hour) and to the Jurassic Coast (½ day). Full day tours, which include time on shore, go to the Isle of Wight, Swanage and Poole. There are evening cruises on most days.

the pier, although only during the main summer tourist seasons and occasionally on bank holidays.

The 693 tonne, 240 feet long, paddle steamer *Waverley* visits Bournemouth every September. She is the last operational sea-going paddle steamer in the world. She was built in 1946 for use on the Clyde and the Scottish Lochs and named after Sir Walter Scott's first novel. The steamer came to the end of her useful life in 1973 and was due be scrapped but was sold for a nominal £1 to the Paddle Steamer Preservation Society. The steamer was fully restored, repainted and given a complete refit. After another rebuild in 2003 she has been restored to her original 1947 condition and now is operational throughout most of the year. The owners claim, probably with justification, that the paddle steamer

Waverley is the most photographed ship in the world. She is licensed to carry up to 800 passengers and has a self-service restaurant, licensed bars, tearoom and souvenir shop. The engine room is particularly worth a visit. The first regular sailings from the pier was in June 1871when the paddle steamer *Heather Belle* sailed to Poole and Swanage.

Cruises from the pier are run by Dorset Cruises Tel: 01202 558550. Tickets for all boat rides and cruises, other than for the *Waverley*, are purchased from the kiosk on **Pier Approach**.

Tickets for rides on the *Waverley* can be purchased by phoning the *Waverley*'s operators (Tel: 0845 130 4647) or on boarding the steamer.

The paddle steamer Waverley.

PIER APPROACH

At the south of the Approach is an amusement arcade, beyond which is the **Pier**. Alongside the arcade is the shop where tickets for boat rides can be purchased and above is the recently opened Aruba bar and restaurant, with views to the pier. The Aruba entrance is to the left of the arcade. There are nearly always a number of children's play activities on Pier Approach, with more of them during the summer season and other holiday periods.

To the east is the East Undercliff **Promenade** and a slip road leading up to the **Russell-Cotes Art Gallery and Museum**.

On the east side of the Approach is the Waterfront Building, once voted the most hated building in the country and it certainly blocks the sea view as visitors drive into Bournemouth. There have been several requests for it to be demolished, including one from the local MP. The building is usually referred to as the IMAX Centre, since it was built to house an IMAX cinema. It cost £20 million to build in 1998 and was due to open the following year but a number of problems beset it and it was not until 2002 that the IMAX finally opened. Even on the opening day it was not possible to show 3D films and only the normal 2D ones were shown. It was shunned by the locals and closed three years later. The cinema equipment has now been removed and that part of the building remains empty. On 20th January 2010 following a full Council meeting the previous day that went on until nearly midnight, the Council bought back the building for £7.5 million and are planning to reduce the height of it. On the first floor of this building is the Harbour Lights pub/restaurant (01202 294307) and on the top floor a coffee shop / toddlers play area. Access to the building is direct from Pier Approach.

To the north, beyond the 1970s'-built traffic flyover, are the award winning **Lower Gardens,** overlooked by the

The Amusement Arcade.

The Waterfront Building.

The Bournemouth International Centre.

Pavilion the entrance of which is in **Westover Road**. The Hot Rocks Café is on the west side of Pier Approach and the slip road to the north of this building leads to the Bournemouth International Centre (BIC) in Exeter Road. The BIC is one of the leading conference and entertainment centres in the world. It was built in 1984 and had a multi-million pound refurbishment in 2005. At the front of the BIC is a statue with Lewis Tregonwell standing holding a tablet commemorating four Victoria Cross holders on one side and Christopher Creeke sitting on a toilet on the other! One of Creeke's many achievements in Bournemouth was to have a proper drainage system installed. He is buried in the **Wimbourne Road Cemetery**.

Backstage tours of the BIC lasting about an hour are held every Thursday from June to September starting at 1400. Booking is recommended (Tel: 0844 5763000). There is a foyer café.

Opposite the BIC is the Punshon Methodist Church which was built in 1958 but closed in 2007 due to lack of worshippers. Further along Exeter Road is the Royal Exeter Hotel which incorporates parts of the Tregonwell's original 1812 villa, such as the central stairs. The villa, known at the time as 'The Mansion' was

Christopher Creeke statue.

Above and left: Royal Exeter Hotel.

The BIC as seen from the Pier.

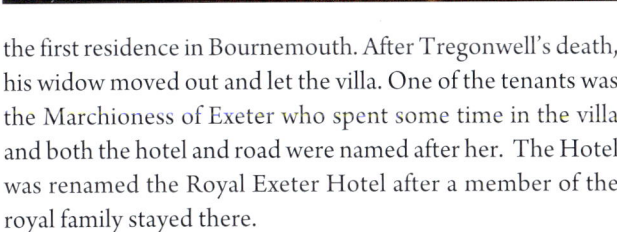

the first residence in Bournemouth. After Tregonwell's death, his widow moved out and let the villa. One of the tenants was the Marchioness of Exeter who spent some time in the villa and both the hotel and road were named after her. The Hotel was renamed the Royal Exeter Hotel after a member of the royal family stayed there.

The path to the south of the Hot Rocks Café leads up to the West Overcliff Promenade past the rear of the BIC. Every Sunday from March to September between 1600 and 1830 a display of classic cars is held here. The cars need to have been registered prior to August 1983 to qualify and the number on display can exceed 100. There is no charge for either

The Hot Rocks Café.

exhibiting or browsing. The event also takes place on New Year's day.

The path continues up to the Marriott Highcliff Hotel, which is one of the top hotels in Bournemouth and where the leaders of the political parties stay when attending their party conference at the BIC. If you look at the manhole covers on the path you will notice the blue seals; before the main political party conferences the drains are inspected for explosive devices and then sealed. The path continues to the **West Overcliff**.

Continuing round Pier Approach, brings you to the **Oceanarium** and then to the West Undercliff **Promenade** going west.

Marriott Highcliff Hotel.

OCEANARIUM

The Oceanarium houses more than 300 species of marine and fresh water creatures from across the globe and attracts around ¼ million visitors a year. Housed on two floors it replicates a number of environments including those at Florida Keys, the Amazon, the Mediterranean, Africa, the Ganges, the Great Barrier Reef and a Tropical Reef.

The Oceanarium runs a captive breeding programme. More than 30 epaulette sharks have been bred from a single breeding pair and the young re-homed in other UK and European aquaria. Similarly more than 15 stingrays have been bred and the Oceanarium was the first aquarium in the UK to breed cownose stingrays. It is also home to creatures rescued by the RSPCA, as can be seen by one of the first exhibits on entering the aquarium, namely the Terrapin Falls, which is now home to a number of terrapins which had grown too large for a home aquarium

The Oceanarium has an interactive 'Global Meltdown' which allows visitors to see the effects of increased sea levels at various dates in the future. It also has the world's first interactive Dive Cage which submerges visitors in a 270° virtual view of the ocean. Interactive touch screens brings visitors up close to various sea creatures through a series of games and challenges. The cage can also be

swallowed by a blue whale so visitors can see its digestive system after which the cage is ejected through the whale's blowhole onto the surface of the ocean.

The Oceanarium has two Green Turtles known as Friday (male) and Crusoe (female) who were re-housed from another aquarium. They are believed to be about 25 years old and in captivity can live to be 150.

Tickets are valid for an entire day so visitors can attend as many of the talks and feedings sessions as they wish. The talks are usually held at 1200 (Stingrays), 1400 (Sharks/Turtles), 1500 (Stingrays) and 1600 (Turtles).

Oceanarium, Pier Approach, West Beach, Bournemouth BH2 5AA. Tel 01202 311993. Open: 1000 – 1700 daily.

The Oceanarium is on the west side of Pier Approach.

THE PROMENADE

The seven miles of soft golden sands have won six seaside awards and four European Blue Flags at *Alum Chine*, Durley Chine, *Fisherman's Walk* and *Southbourne*. The promenade extends as far as the Sandbanks Hotel on the west and to *Southbourne and Fisherman's Walk* on the east. The beaches have to be constantly maintained and replenished as the sand retreats into the sea. In 1907 the sea wall, groynes and promenade were built to stop the erosion of the cliffs. This work was successful but a side effect was that the sea no longer deposited sand on the shore and so has to be regularly topped up. This was last done in 2007 and immediately afterwards the beach was the widest it had been for 60 years but already the sand has retreated significantly. There is a natural west to east movement of the costal waters which means that if left to nature the finer sand will be at Sandbanks and the coarser particles at Hengistbury Head. In fact the beach is 90% sand around Bournemouth Pier and only 35% sand around Hengistbury Head.

During the summer period, the Land Train operates from the pier and travels to *Alum Chine* to the west and *Boscombe* Pier to the east during holiday periods and many weekends.

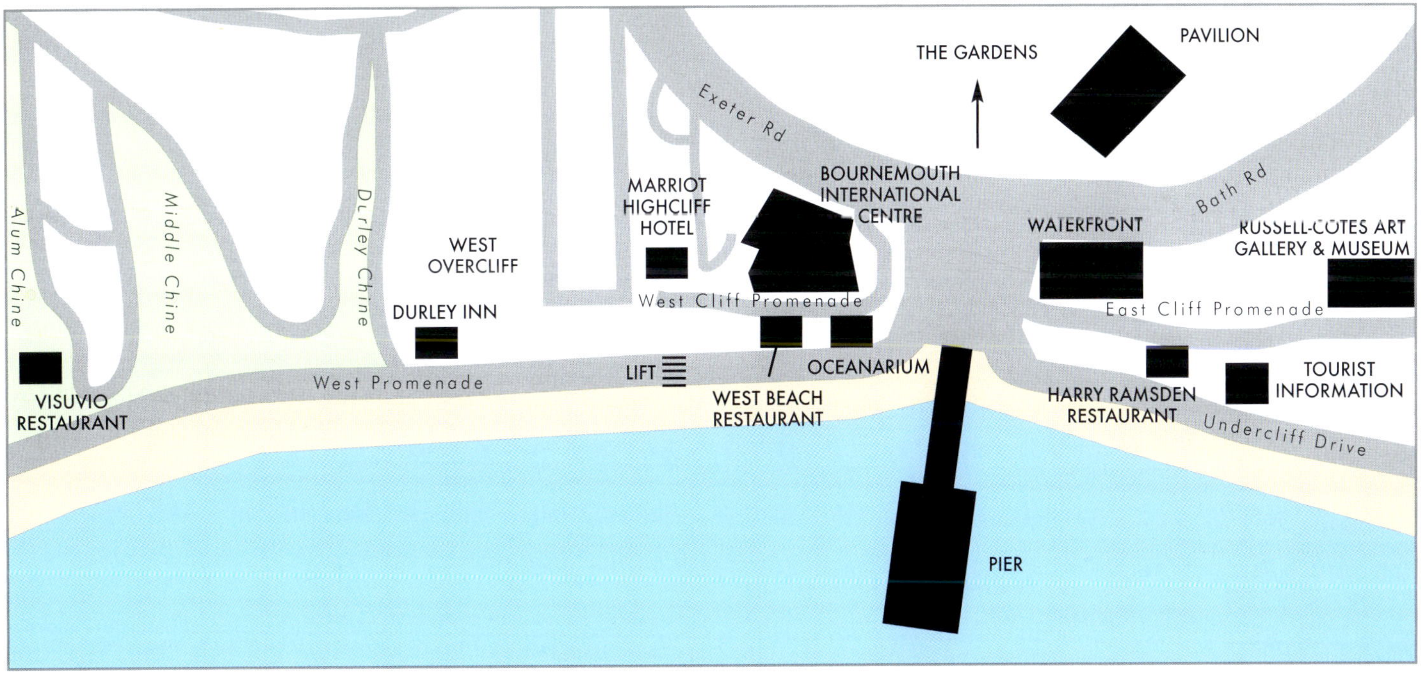

THE GARDENS

PAVILION

Exeter Rd

Bath Rd

MARRIOT HIGHCLIFF HOTEL

BOURNEMOUTH INTERNATIONAL CENTRE

WATERFRONT

RUSSELL-COTES ART GALLERY & MUSEUM

Alum Chine

Middle Chine

Durley Chine

WEST OVERCLIFF

DURLEY INN

West Cliff Promenade

East Cliff Promenade

LIFT

WEST BEACH RESTAURANT

OCEANARIUM

HARRY RAMSDEN RESTAURANT

TOURIST INFORMATION

West Promenade

Undercliff Drive

VISUVIO RESTAURANT

PIER

Bournemouth was the first resort to operate a 'Kids Safety' scheme. From July to September, parents can collect a free wristband for their children from any of the six beach offices. They then can write their mobile phone number on the wrist band and place them on their child's wrist. Should parents and children become separated, the uniformed officials are informed and then up to 120 officials who work on the beach front at any one time can quickly search for the missing child.

Dogs are excluded from large areas of the beach between 1 May and 30 September but they are allowed on the beach at **Alum Chine**, Durley Chine and from **Southbourne** to **Hengistbury Head**.

Bournemouth has three cliff lifts, one on the East Cliff, another on the West Cliff and a third at **Fisherman's Walk**. The correct name for them is 'funicular railway' or 'funicular tramway'. They are operated by a driver at the top controlling the winding gear and an assistant at the bottom. All have the same gauge of 5½ feet and all the carriages are interchangeable. The original carriages were made of wood but these were replaced by aluminium in the 1960s. The first lift to be built in Bournemouth was the East Cliff Railway which opened in April 1908. It has the longest track of the three with a

length of 170 feet. In August of the same year the West Cliff Railway, with a length of 145 feet, opened leading to the Highcliff Marriott Hotel. The Fisherman's Walk Railway opened in 1935. It is the shortest of the three with a length of 128 feet and leads to **Fisherman's Walk** and **Boscombe**. All three lifts give good views to Purbeck and the Isle of Wight.

Hours of operation are from 0915 – 1815. They only operate during the summer and at other holiday periods. It costs more to ascend than to descend!

Beach huts (see page 119) can be hired for the day or for longer, although there is a waiting list for lets covering a full season. There are over 250 to chose from. Costs vary on location, time of year and duration of let. 24 new ones are for sale at Alum Chine costing around £40,000 for a 25 year lease and 31 in **Boscombe Spa Village**

costing from £65,000 to £90,000. (Tel: 01202 451781 or visit the Beach Office just east of Bournemouth Pier). Kayaks can be hired from beside the pier. (Tel: 07970 971867).

Westover and Bournemouth Rowing Club (WBRC), founded in 1865, is the oldest club in Bournemouth. In the past there was a convention that the prospective local MP should purchase a boat for the club; this custom lapsed many years ago to the relief of the current MPs. The club is unusual in that members row on the sea, unlike most other clubs where rowing takes place on rivers. The members of WBRC claim river rowing is for 'wimps'. In fact the only place in the world where costal rowing is undertaken is on the South Coast of England. Compared with river boats, costal boats have a wider bottom, are shorter and the seats are staggered, all of which adds to stability. The boats take one, two or four rowers. The club's

best boats are more than 40 years old. Rowing takes place every evening from May to September between 1830 and 2030 with races on Saturdays at different locations along the south coast. The Council has plans to re-locate the club and redevelop the site.

There are a number of eating places along the Promenade, including four main restaurants, all of which get very busy at peak times. The restaurants are: Vesuvio Bar Restaurant at Alum Chine (Tel: 01202 759100), Durley Inn at Durley Chine (Tel: 01202 290480); West Beach Restaurant just west of the pier (live jazz on Thursdays from 2000; Tel: 01202 587785) and Harry Ramsden Fish Restaurant just east of the pier (01202 295818)

The Sea Front Office of the Tourist Centre is a short way to the east of the pier. (Tel: 01202 451781)

From the beginning of the school holidays to the end of August, depending on whether the Council can find a sponsor, there may be a firework display from the pier on Friday evenings starting at 2200 and lasting for ten minutes. The fireworks are ignited on a barge just off the east side of the pier. About thirty minutes before the start of the display, the bay around the pier fills with pleasure craft. The pier lights are dimmed immediately before the start. The display can be viewed from anywhere on the beaches or cliff tops. A good way to view it is to take the Bournemouth Eye Balloon, which goes up about five minutes before the display and descends about 30 minutes later.

There is a display held off Sandbanks every Thursday evening starting at 2230, again from the start of the school holidays to the end of August. Because the display takes place off the beach, it can

The commemorative stone erected on the opening of the Undercliff Drive in 1907.

readily be seen from Bournemouth, to the west of the pier and in particular from the **West Overcliff**. A sunset cruise departs from Bournemouth Pier at 1930 that goes to Poole Harbour and then returns for a grandstand view of the display. There are a number of displays to see on or around 5 November – ask the Tourist Information Centre for details. One of the best must be that at Poole's Quay, not least because it is free! It is billed as the biggest free event on the South Coast, although Bournemouth's Air Festival surely has that honour. The entertainment starts at around 1630 with a number of performers. The firework display itself starts at 1945.

WEST OVERCLIFF

The West Overcliff is a lawned leisure area with good views of the Isle of Wight to the east and the Purbeck Hills to the west. Light refreshments can be purchased in the gardens of either the Marriott Highcliff or Rivera Hotels. The path along the cliff top leads through a small copse, where squirrels can normally be seen, to steps leading down to Durley Chine and the Durley Inn.

Beacon Road to the west of the BIC leads to the Bourne Beat Hotel (Tel:01202 553319) on the corner with Priory Road. Here there is a real taste of 1960s' nostalgia as the hotel has a host of original photos, posters, etc of the 1960s' stars such as Andy Williams, Cliff Richards, The Shadows, Tom Jones and many others.

One of the zig-zag paths leading to the beach.

A commemorative stone for the site of a Bronze Age Barrow (burial site).

Path along the cliff top.

Admirals Walk.

The doors open at 1930, with a meal at 2030. Rubyz Cabaret Restaurant, 101 West Hill Road, Bournemouth, BH2 5EB (opposite the Connaught Hotel). Tel 01202 552553.

Rubyz Cabaret Restaurant.

Overlooking the West Overcliff is one of the town's premier apartment blocks known as Admirals Walk. The block was built in the 1970s and little is known of how its name arose. The history of Admirals Walk is not clear. The Ordnance Survey map of 1870 shows an empty plot. A home known as Western Hall was built on the site in 1947 and was later replace by a hotel of the same name. It is said that an admiral lived in Western Hall and a path to the cliff top received its name because he walked daily to the sea. A Blue Plaque in honour of the astronomer Sir Fred Hoyle, who lived in Admirals Walk for some years, was unveiled in December 2009.

St Michael's Road and West Hill Road, to the west of the Marriott Highcliff Hotel leads to several hotels, restaurants, cafés, pubs plus a small general store. On St Michael's Road is Rubyz Cabaret Restaurant. This is located in an old listed church building that has been carefully converted. If you happen to be in town when there is a show then don't miss it; their resident drag queen, Miss Kitty, is excellent. Downstairs is a large bar and seating for pre-dinner drinks while the eating area on the first floor has retained many of the building's original features.

A horrific murder took place in the area in 1946 when Group Captain Rupert Brooke, who was staying at the Tollard Royal Hotel (now Tollard Court), murdered Doreen Marshall. Her body was found in Durley Chine with her throat cut and her body mutilated and slashed. It was a replica of another murder that had taken place in London near to where Brooke lived. His defence lawyer argued that Brooke must be insane to have carried out such a murder but the jury found him guilty. On the way to the gallows he asked the prison Governor for a double whisky!

The West Overcliff is reached from the beach by taking the West Cliff lift to the Marriott Highcliff Hotel, or walking up one of the zigzag paths, or walking up from Pier Approach to the left of the Hot Rocks Café.

THE LOWER GARDENS

The gardens at the heart of Bournemouth extend for nearly two miles and are divided into three parts. The area from Pier Approach to the Square is the Lower Gardens, from the Square to Wessex Way Flyover is the Central Gardens and the Upper Gardens are from Wessex Way to Havelock Road, which is actually in Poole.

The gardens were laid out towards the end of the 19th century, prior to then the Bourne Valley was marshy. Major changes to the Lower Gardens were made in the 1920s when the Pavilion was built and the Square was created which divided the Lower and Central Gardens. The rockery in front of the Pavilion was also created at that time. Apart from these changes most of the gardens seen today are as they were in the 1870s. The River Bourne passes through the gardens but it is taken underground as it enters the sea.

The flower beds are well-stocked throughout the year but during the summer there are brilliant colourful displays of bedding plants, including one bed depicting Bournemouth's Coat of Arms. Each year the arrangements are different. In 2006, Chris Evans, who is responsible for designing the gardens, won a Gold Medal at the Chelsea Flower Show together with the coveted President's Award; this is the first time that both awards have been won at the same time by the

The Crazy Golf course was refurbished in 2008.

same exhibitor. Also in the Lower Gardens is a range of activities throughout the year but particularly during the summer season. During the summer holidays there is a Kids Fun Festival offering free entertainment for children. On most Wednesday evenings during August the 100 year old 'Candle Illuminations' tradition is held when 1000s of coloured candles are lit throughout the Lower Gardens.

For details of the programme and times contact the Tourist Information Centre.

Bournemouth's 'Concert in the Gardens' runs from June to September when on most days there is a band or orchestra playing in the Bandstand.

In the Lower Gardens during the summer season is the Bournemouth Eye, which is a tethered balloon. Tethered ballooning was pioneered by the Victorians and became very popular towards the end of the 19th century. The balloon is filled with helium and rises to a height of 500ft from where (weather permitting) panoramic views of Bournemouth, Poole Harbour, the Isle of Wight, the New Forest and the English Channel can be seen. The tether is a strong steel cable; the gondola holds up to 30 people. Passenger certificates are available at the end of the ride. By law, flights cannot take place if the wind speed exceeds 30 knots, although rain is not a handicap. You are advised to phone to check weather conditions if you intend flying and the weather is uncertain.

Rides take place every day from Easter to the end of September, from 0730 – 2300, weather permitting. Tickets are purchased from the kiosk in the gardens near the Square. The Eye is wheelchair accessible. Tel: 01202 314539.

The Bournemouth Eye.

The Welsh limestone rockery in front of the Pavilion has recently been restored with some unusual species of plants associated more with Mediterranean countries and South Africa. The rockery is the largest municipal rockery in the UK. It was constructed in 1930 and now has Grade II listed status.

PREVIOUS PAGE
View of the northern end of the Lower Gardens as seen from the Exeter Road in front of Debenhams Department Store.

The aviary was built in 1919 and was originally thatched.

Hand-worked jewellery stand.

In the east of the gardens is Pinewalk which is directly accessible from **Westover Road**. 'Pinewalk' used to be known as 'Invalids Walk' since the aroma from the pine trees was considered by the Victorians to have healing benefits. Today the trees are very dense and consideration is being given to thinning them so that there will be a clear view to the sea once again.

Bournemouth's open air art exhibition, referred to as 'The Gallery in the Gardens', claims to be the largest open air art display outside

In front of the aviary is a small outdoor café.

of London, and is where independent artists display their work for sale. The exhibition in Pinewalk has been running for more than 50 years. The work on display is mainly paintings and photography although there is hand-worked jewellery for sale and any form of art work could be displayed.

The exhibition runs from late May to early September and is open from 0930 – 1700. Further details can be obtained by phoning 01202 451718.

WESTOVER ROAD

Overlooking Westover Road at the south end is the Royal Bath Hotel. It was built for Sir George Gervis and was Bournemouth's first hotel. It was known at the time as the Bath Hotel and opened for the first time on Queen Victoria's coronation day, 28 June 1838. The Russell-Cotes purchased the hotel in 1876 and extensively refurbished and enlarged it before opening it as the Royal Bath Hotel in 1880. Among the famous people who have stayed there have been the future King Edward VII, Oscar Wilde and Benjamin Disraeli.

Westover Road runs alongside the Lower Gardens and the only buildings on the south side of the road are the Pavilion and the Tourist Information Centre. On the north side are a number of high quality boutiques, a casino, two multi-screen cinemas and a state-of-the-art laser entertainment centre. This road was at one time referred to as the Bond Street of Bournemouth and will in the foreseeable future regain its former glory as the Council are planning a major regeneration of the area.

Bournemouth's 'Bond Street'.

Entrance to Pine Walk.

At the end of Westover Road is the Tourist Information Centre (Tel: 0845 0511700). It is worth buying a copy of 'What's On' which costs a nominal amount. This gives details of all the shows and concerts, events, exhibitions, talks and lectures and markets & fairs for the month. The first Tourist Information Centre was built on the site in the 1930s and was paid for by the Chamber of Commerce.

To the right at the end of Westover Road is **St Peter's Church**, directly ahead through the Arcade (built in 1866) is the pedestrian shopping area, while to the left is Gervis Place (where most of the town's buses stop), with the **Square** at its far end.

THE PAVILION

The Pavilion was officially opened on 19 March 1929. Before the Pavilion was built the Belle Vue Boarding House was on the site and from 1861 had been home to Bournemouth's first Catholic chapel. The Pavilion was initially built as a concert hall to house the Municipal Orchestra (later to become the Bournemouth Symphony Orchestra) and the stage was only added four years later. The Compton Organ was installed during the building of the theatre. There are 17 dressing rooms which can accommodate 150 people. The ballroom is the largest in the South of England. The auditorium is on two levels and can seat 1500. There is a revolving stage and the orchestra pit can be raised and lowered. Over the years there have been a number of additions and changes to the building and a multi-million-pound redevelopment of the Pavilion was due to start in 2009 but delays have arisen due to the uncertainty about rights over parts of the land. In the meantime the Council are investing more than £3 million for the creation of a Dance Centre in one of the vacant rooms with the aim of making Bournemouth the dance capital of the south of England. Over the years there have been several calls for the building to be demolished but its future is now secure after it was Grade II listed in 1998. Many of the great names in show-business have performed here over the years.

Back stage tours lasting 60–90 minutes are held every Friday from June to September. Booking for these tours is recommended. (Tel: 0844 5763000).

WINTER GARDENS AND THE BOURNEMOUTH SYMPHONY ORCHESTRA

The first Winter Gardens was built in 1877 and was modelled on London's Crystal Palace. It was Bournemouth's first public theatre and was a mainly glass building. It was replaced by a brick building in 1937 which was designed as an indoor bowling green. Fortunately the building had brilliant acoustics and was soon converted into a 2000 seat concert hall and became home to the BSO until it was demolished in 2006. The site is currently used as a car park but there are plans to have temporary family attractions there from summer 2010.

The Bournemouth Symphony Orchestra (BSO) was originally known as the Bournemouth Municipal Orchestra and was founded in 1893 by Dan Godfrey, who remained its Principal Conductor for the next 31 years. It is the oldest full-time orchestra in the country. Initially it only played military music on the Pier although it soon developed into a full orchestra but did not change its name to the BSO until 1954. The orchestra is Internationally known and performs regularly in the BBC Proms as well as at overseas venues, such as the Carnegie Hall in New York. Its conductors have included Elgar, Holst, Sibelius and Stravinsky who all conducted their own works, as well as prominent conductors such as Silvestri. The BSO gave its first concert in the Winter Gardens in 1893. The location was not ideal since if it rained heavily the noise on the glass roof drowned out the music! The BSO moved its base to the Pavilion Theatre when it opened in 1929,

then back to the new Winter Gardens when it opened again in 1947 and finally when the Winter Gardens closed, to the Poole Lighthouse Theatre, where it is currently based. It still gives performances in Bournemouth (Tel: 01202 669925).

Dan Godfrey was buried in **St Peter's Church's** graveyard; over 1000 people attended his funeral. Next to his grave is a memorial stone to Constantin Silvestri who was the Principal Conductor of the BSO from 1961–1969.

ST PETER'S CHURCH

In 1841 work began on building a church and was completed three years later. When it was first completed the building was considered so unattractive and the inside so bare that nobody could initially be found to be the vicar and the Bishop of Winchester refused to consecrate it until one had been found. The church finally opened a year later in summer 1845 when the Rev. Bennett accepted the post. Rev. Bennett proved a man of great energy, vision and religious conviction; during his time at the church he established six church schools, as well as enlarging and improving the church, which was completed in 1879. He held the service of thanksgiving in December of that year and died one month later; he is buried in the churchyard. St Peter's is now one of the finest Victorian buildings in the country and has Grade I listing.

Rev. Bennett was fortunate in having some wealthy benefactors and he used the finest workmanship available at the time. The font and pulpit are examples of their work. The latter was displayed in the Great International Exhibition in London in 1862 before being transferred to St Peter's; it is said to be the finest Victorian pulpit in the country.

Next to the steps at the rear of the church is a plan showing the location of some of the important memorials in the graveyard The

Tregonwell Family Tomb contains the remains of Lewis Tregonwell (the founder of Bournemouth), together with his wife, son and four other family members. Lewis Tregonwell died before the church was built but his wife had his body transferred here from the family vault in Winterbourne Anderson.

Mary Shelley, the author of the Frankenstein story, is buried here, along with her mother, father, son and heart of her poet husband Percy. Percy was drowned during a violent storm when travelling by boat off the coast of Italy in 1822. His remains were later washed

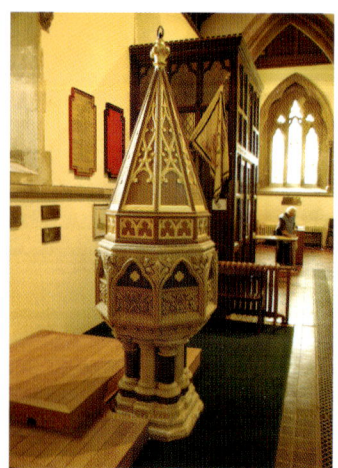

ghost stories. She wrote the novel, published in 1818, when she was only 19. Mary's mother, Mary Wollstonecraft, is depicted on a 2009 Royal Mail stamp. She was a major writer at the time and published *A Vindication of the Rights of Women* in which she argued that women should have equal education rights to men. She died in 1797 as a result of giving birth to her daughter and her body was later removed from its original burial place in London to the family tomb. There are murals to Mary in the Mary Shelley pub, opposite the church.

The church has one of the best non-cathedral choirs in the country; a girls choir was established for the first time in 2009. It has one of the finest organs on the south coast as well as a Steinway grand piano. Lunchtime concerts are held on Wednesday afternoons starting at 1315 from Easter to Christmas. The type of music varies and includes gospel, church, blues, classical and opera. The church's coffee shop is open throughout the year Monday to Friday from 1030 – 1400.

St Peter's Church, Hinton Road, Bournemouth BH1 2EE
Tel: 01202 290986

Turn right at the end of **Westover Road** and St Peter's Church is directly ahead of you.

ashore and his badly decomposed body was cremated on the beach. However his heart was saved from the funeral pyre by one of his friends and then was kept by Mary, pressed flat in a copy of one of her husband's books. There is controversy as to how much input Percy had in the writing of *Frankenstien*, with claims varying from little to a lot. The idea for the monster is said to have arisen when Mary, her husband–to–be and Lord Byron spent an evening together telling

THE SQUARE

The origins of the Square probably date back to 1849 when a bridge was built over the Bourne Stream where the Square now is. The Square is usually full of activity with events taking place every weekend, as well as on many weekdays especially during the holiday periods. At Christmas there is a European Market, during summer a children's play area and at other times often different groups of musicians.

In the centre of the Square is the continental style Obscura Café. On its first floor is one of the world's largest viewing cameras, namely a Camera Obscura. It acts like a large periscope and projects an image of the outside onto a circular horizontal screen in the centre of a darkened room. The outside clock tower, holding the periscope, can rotate by 360° and so give all-round viewing. The camera has not operated for some time but is due to do so again in April 2010. There will be set times for the show but will be highly dependent on the weather. During the show the blinds will be lowered and the room darkened. There is also a monitor showing archive pictures of Bournemouth and it is intended to have an up-market menu available for those who want to eat there. The first floor has good views over the square.

Obscura Café, The Square, Bournemouth BH2 6EG. Tel: 01202 314231

To the west of the café is Debenhams Department Store. On this site in 1838 there were two semi-detached cottages which were knocked into one to become a place of worship – the first in Bournemouth. After *St Peter's Church* was built, the cottages were pulled down and the materials were sold to Miss Talbot who used them in the building of *Talbot Village*.

The former St Andrew's United Reformed Church.

The road to the left of Debenhams passes in front of the Moon in the Square public house and then to the V-club. Until quite recently this was the St Andrew's United Reformed Church. Due to falling numbers of worshippers the church closed in 2005 and members joined the Richmond Hill United Reformed Church. The building is Grade II listed. The V-club has music at weekends and live entertainment on occasions during the week. Up to April 2009 it was known as the Landmarc Bar & Restaurant.

The pedestrian walkway to the right of Debenhams leads to a major shopping area, including Marks & Spencers, BHS and a range of smaller shops. A few shops past Debenhams is the Build-a-Bear-Workshop (Tel: 01202 559126) where children can make their own teddybear. At the top of the hill and to the right is the area known as the Triangle. Here is the town's main library which opened in spring 2002 (Tel: 01202 454848). The building won the prestigious Prime Minister's Better Public Buildings Award in 2003 and was the first public library to win such a National Award. There is also a number of adult shops and gay clubs in the area. The Triangle is to be trans-

formed into a public park and entertainment area. Returning to the Square, on the north-east corner of **Richmond Hill** is the NatWest Bank. It was built in 1888 and the history of it, including its use as a hotel, is given on the Blue Plaque on the front of the building.

BOURNE AVENUE

Bourne Avenue goes along the north side of Central Gardens and has a number of cafés, restaurants and coffee shops. At the All Fired Up Ceramics Café visitors can choose any ceramic item from the large range available and decorate it to their own design using the pencils, stamps and paint provided. The fired item can be collected a few days later.

Richmond Hill St Andrew's United Reformed Church.

All Fired Up Ceramics Café, The Square, 35 – 37 Bourne Avenue, Bournemouth, BH2 6DT Tel: 01202 558030. Open: Monday to Saturday, 0930 – 1800 (2200 on Thursday and Friday) and 1030 – 1630 on Sundays

Continuing along Bourne Avenue on the right is Richmond Hill St Andrew's United Reformed Church which is the largest church in Bournemouth, capable of seating 1200 worshippers. The first permanent church on the site held its first service on 8 March 1859 but soon became too small for its congregation and was replaced by the present church in 1891. It has come to be known as the Cathedral of Congregationalism. One of the church's most treasured features is the beautiful stained glass South window which depicts scenes from the Knights of the Round Table and the Quest for the Holy Grail. Also of note are the concentric curved pews and the Tapestry 2000 which was created over a period of 14 months by members of the church to mark the millennium. Typical of many congregational churches is the dominant nature of the beautiful pulpit with its stone carvings which was a gift from the minister, Rev. Ossian Davies, at the time the church was built. The church's organ is one of the best in the Borough and organ concerts are held during the months of July and August.

The church is open from 1000 – 1200 on Thursdays (Tel: 01202 290161)

Beyond the United Reformed Church is Bournemouth's Town Hall. The foundation stone was laid by the King of Sweden and Norway in 1881 and opened as the ultra-luxury Monte Dore Hotel in 1885. It is now a Grade II listed building. During the First World War the hotel was requisitioned to be used as a hospital for the wounded and subsequently a convalescent home for British Officers. It was purchased by Bournemouth Council and became their Town Hall in 1921. The table and sideboards in the Mayor's Parlour are thought to have originally been in Highcliff Castle.

Bournemouth's Town Hall.

CENTRAL AND UPPER GARDENS

In contrast to the Lower Gardens, the Central and Upper Gardens are places of peace and tranquillity. Surprisingly few tourists visit them and the Council is hoping to attract more visitors to these areas. An excellent new woodland-style play area has been created, known as the Jurassic Play Jungle, with a play-house slide, nest swing, climbing frame with cargo nets and zip line. Unfortunately the Council forgot to apply for the necessary planning permission at the time and had to apply for it retrospectively.

The herbaceous border between the Pergola and the War Memorial presents a colourful display during July and August. The Tennis Courts beyond the War Memorial were relocated from the Upper Gardens in 1903.

The Water Tower in the Upper Gardens between Queens Road and Prince of Wales Road, was built sometime between 1865 and 1885 in the style of a medieval castle with battlements and a crenellated turret. Water was pumped into the tower by a waterwheel powered by the Bourne Stream and the water was used to irrigate the gardens. The wheel itself and workings were removed in 1940 for armaments. The site of the wheel was 50 yards downstream where there is now a weir. The tower is home to a number of bats as part of the town's environmental conservation programme.

The War Memorial was built in 1922 to commemorate those who fell in the First World War. The two lions guarding the Memorial are copies of the two lions guarding the tomb of Pope Clement XIII in St Peter's Basilica, Rome.

The Pergola was built in 1990 to commemorate the centenary of the Borough of Bournemouth.

The Water Tower in the Upper Gardens.

Much of the gardens used to be marsh land and even today the Central and Upper Gardens can flood and are frequently waterlogged.

Beyond Queens Road there are several gravel paths and board walks some of which cross the River Bourne that flows throughout the length of the gardens.

In 1874 nearly 4000 trees and shrubs were planted representing the taste of the Victorians at the time. There is a Tree Trail throughout the 2 mile length of the gardens and a leaflet can be obtained from the Tourist Information Office or phone 01202 437812. Although the trail starts in the Lower Gardens most of the trees mentioned are in the Central and Upper Gardens. The trees include ones from Persia and Japan

At the end of the Upper Gardens is Coy Pond, which is actually in Poole. 'Coy' is short for 'De-Coy' and the history books tell us that the pond was built to act as a decoy for birds which could then be shot for sport. However the information board at the pond supplied by the Council denies this. The pond is not actually in the gardens but on the north side of Coy Pond Road. Being at the end of the Chine the area used to be a storage point for contraband brought up from

Coy Pond.

Bourne Bottom (where the Pier now is) through the Chine by the smugglers and then distributed. The pond provided a convenient dumping ground for the contraband if the customs officers were coming close.

There is limited street parking in Bourne Avenue so you could join the Central Gardens close to the War Memorial or tennis courts and walk north or walk south from Coy Pond Road (Post Code BH12 1JT) where there is street parking.

RICHMOND HILL

Richmond Hill which exits from the northeast side of The Square, is home to a number of Bournemouth's oldest and most commanding buildings, many of which have listed status. A few yards down Post Office Road, which is the first road on the right, is the old Post Office Building vacated by the Post Office in 2007 when they moved to W H Smith in Gervis Road. The building is currently unoccupied and for sale. Further down and on the opposite side of the road to the post office is R E Porter, the oldest established jeweller and silversmith in Bournemouth. On the corner of Richmond Hill and Post Office Road is the Roman Catholic Church of the Sacred Heart. A small wooden Roman Catholic church was opened on Richmond Hill in 1869. Four years later a small brick church had been built on the present site. However no

sooner had it been opened than it was too small and a new enlarged building opened in 1875. A bell was added to the new bell tower later the same year; this was one of the few Catholic churches at the time to have a bell since they had been banned prior to the Emancipation Act of 1829. Over the next 12 years the church was further enlarged and was completed in its present form in 1888.

Opposite the Church is the Norfolk Royale Hotel. Two large villas which had been built between 1840 and 1850 were joined in 1870 to form Stewarts Hotel. The building was enlarged in 1903 and a cast-iron, art nouveau veranda added. The name was changed in 1910 to the Norfolk Hotel in recognition of the fact that the Duke and Duchess of Norfolk regularly stayed in the hotel during the summers at that time. As they were Roman Catholics it was

Left and above: The Roman Catholic Church of the Sacred Heart.

convenient for them to be able to attend the Sacred Heart Church opposite. The hotel's name was changed again to the Norfolk Royale Hotel when a further enlargement was carried out in 1988 with the building of an additional block along St Stephen's Road. The building achieved listed status in 1974. The hotel's suites are given the names of the Duke of Norfolk's titles, namely the Arundel (held by the Duke in 1139), Beaumont (in 1309), Maltravers (in 1330) and Surrey (in 1483). The current Duke holds all these titles.

Above and left: The Norfolk Royale Hotel.

The art-deco-style Daily Echo *print room.*

On the corner of Albert Road is the art-deco-style, *Daily Echo* print room which was purpose built for the newspaper in 1934 and now has Grade II listing. With the onset of modern technology such a large building was no longer required and from the early 1990s it was largely empty. It has now been turned into a restaurant appropriately called 'The Print Room'. The spacious and imposing interior won the 'Best New Interior' British Design Award when it opened in 2007. Next to it along Albert Road is the pink façade of the rear of the old Theatre Royal

A short way further up the hill on the left is St Stephen's Road. Along this road is one of Bournemouth's mosques on the left and next to it is the entrance to Richmond Hill St Andrew's United Reformed Church. Further along the road is **St Stephen's Church**.

The Print Room Bar and Brassiere, Richmond Hill, Bournemouth, BH2 6HH. Tel: 01202 789669. Open from 0800 – 2400.

The old Theatre Royal.

Curzon Casino.

THE THEATRE ROYAL 1882
1887 ONWARDS USED AS TOWN
HALL 1892 - THEATRE ROYAL, 1939
SERVICES CLUB, 1949 - NEW
THEATRE, ROYAL, 1959 - OPERA
HOUSE, 1962 - CINEMA, 1963 -
BINGO HALL, 1971 - CINEMA CLUB,
1985
CURZON CASINO
SPORTING CLUB

Granville Chambers.

Returning to Richmond Hill, on the right is Yelverton Road and the Curzon Casino. It has been said that Bournemouth once had more theatres than London. While this is probably not true it certainly has had a number over the years. The first was a private one built by Sir Percy Shelley in 1849 for himself and his invited guests. Later he opened it to the public and gave proceedings of performances to local charities. The oldest theatre still in Bournemouth was the Theatre Royal in Yelverton Road which opened in December 1882 and seated 800. Since then and before becoming a casino the building has had various uses as can be seen from the blue plaque on the wall.

The Granville Chambers on the corner with Yelverton Road was built in 1891 as a Temperance Hotel. From 1900 – 1930 it was the Granville Hotel. Since 1930 the building has been used as offices (mainly as the head office of Beales Department Store), with major refurbishments carried out in 1985.

ST STEPHEN'S CHURCH

St Stephen's church was built between 1881 and 1898 as a memorial to Rev. Bennett, the first vicar of **St Peter's Church.** After the death of Rev. Bennett in 1879 it was thought that St Peter's would revert to the old style Church of England Worship, rather than the High Anglicanism which he had introduced. His son therefore set about the construction of St Stephen's and employed John Pearson, consider to be finest church builder at the time who also designed Truro and Brisbane Cathedrals. He designed both the main building and the internal fixtures, commenting at the time 'I wish to design a church that will bring people to their knees'. In this it is generally considered that he succeeded. John Betjeman described it as one of the most beautiful churches in England and

Simon Jenkins in his book *England's Thousand Best Churches* describes it as 'a masterpiece'. It is one of only three Grade I listed buildings in Bournemouth. The exterior is relatively plain and can be seen to lack a spire. Although one was planned it was never built. Note the carving over the south porch, which represents Christ, and that over the west door, which represents St Stephen.

The bowl of the font is cut from a single piece of Italian marble. The marble pulpit depicts Jesus preaching the Sermon on the Mount, St Peter preaching at Pentecost and St Paul preaching in Athens. To the right of the Chancel is a statue of St Stephen who was the first Christian martyr to be stoned to death; he is holding a stone in his right hand. The church is famous for its large choir and each summer a series of concerts are held of music by Mozart, Haydn and Schubert.

St Stephen's Church, St Stephen's Way, Bournemouth BH2 6JZ.

Walk north along Braidley Road along the side of the Town Hall. The steps just before the flyover lead to the church.

RUSSELL-COTES ART GALLERY AND MUSEUM

This small art gallery and museum, located on the East Cliff in a large Victorian villa overlooking the sea, is a joy to behold. The villa, originally known as East Cliff Hall, is one of the few Victorian villas remaining in Bournemouth and, following extensive refurbishment between 1998 and 2001, can be seen today much the same as when it was built. The building, which is of national importance, was completed in 1901, which is the year Queen Victoria died and so is one of the last Victorian buildings to have been built. It was opened as the Art Gallery and Museum by the Lord Mayor of London on 5 June 1909. The building was designed and lived in by Sir Merton and Lady Russell-Cotes and its interior is described as 'flamboyant' and 'eccentric'. Many of the exhibits reflect the tastes of that time and were collected by the owners during their world travels. Sir Merton and his wife gifted the Hall and all its contents, to Bournemouth Borough Council in 1909. Merton Russell-Cotes is the only Mayor of Bournemouth who was not also a member of the Council. He found the first Council meeting he chaired to be so stressful that he gave the chairing of future meetings to his deputy!

The art gallery has a world-renowned Japanese collection and the museum frequently lends objects for exhibiting elsewhere; part of its Japanese collection was recently lent to the Japanese Embassy to commemorate the 150th anniversary of the opening of formal diplomatic relations between Japan and the UK.

The Irving Room hosts a collection dedicated to the great Shakespearean actor, Sir Henry Irving and includes the skull he used in playing Hamlet.

Among the museum's many prized possessions are the bureau used by Napoleon Bonaparte during his exile in St Helena, as well as his dining table and lamp. Sir Merton, who was of similar build to Napoleon, used the table as a desk in its current position under the beautiful stained glass windows. A cabinet displays some of the silver-gilt wedding gifts given to the Mertons and adjacent to it is a large display bureau that used to belong to Empress Eugénie, wife of Napoleon III. After the Emperor and his wife had fled their palace the contents of it were dispersed and Sir Merton purchased the bureau from a dealer in London. When Empress Eugénie saw the cabinet on a subsequent visit to the Russell-Cotes, she is reported to have

swooned. She is said to have later given them a diamond ring, no doubt hoping for the return of the bureau, but in fact Sir Merton kept both the ring and the bureau.

The museum has an extensive collection of over 80,000 objects or groups of objects in its store and has enquiries and visits from people from many countries, in particular Japan and America. Seriously interested parties can visit the store but only by prior appointment. There is a small café where all the items, such as furniture, curtains and tableware have been designed by local artists.

Russell-Cotes Art Gallery & Museum, East Cliff, Bournemouth, BH1 3AA. Tel: 01202 451858. Open: Daily from 1000 – 1700. Closed on Mondays. Free Admission.

Walk up past the Royal Bath Hotel, turn right along Russell Cotes Road and the Art Gallery and Museum is a few yards along on the right. Alternatively walk up the East Cliff Promenade from Pier Approach. The entrance currently being used is the one in East Cliff Promenade.

The cemetery chapel.

WIMBORNE ROAD CEMETERY

Cemeteries, unlike churchyards and graveyards, are not linked with a regular place of worship and are usually multi-denominational. Bournemouth's main cemetery is at Wimborne Road and was opened in 1878. Its history and importance are recognised by its inclusion on the Register of Parks and Gardens and is Grade II listed. The cemetery chapel, built of Purbeck Stone, is in two parts. The west side is not consecrated and is for use by people of all faiths. The beautiful stained windows in this part were donated by the Russell-Cotes in 1907.

The chapel on the east side is consecrated but has been allowed to fall into a state of disrepair and is not normally open to the public. There are plans to restore it, hopefully with the aid of a lottery grant, with the small vestry turned into a toilet. This chapel, which in many ways is the prettiest of the two chapels, could then be used to hold meetings. Significant repairs are required to the main building and these are due to start in April 2010. The several Monkey Puzzle trees (Chilean Pines) were given to the cemetery by nurseryman Joseph Cutler. Subsequently the Victorians associated the trees with death and would not buy any from him. As a consequence he went bankrupt.

The building closest to the chapel is the Russell-Cotes Mausoleum which is open to the public by prior appointment. It is hoped that a Friends of Wimborne Road Cemetery can be formed in the near future which would permit the mausoleum to be open at regular times

The small mortuary is in a sad state of repair and the Council had plans to demolish it. However an application has been made to English Heritage for the building to be listed. As can be seen from the east side, the building has cavity walls and is one of the earliest examples of such work. There is said to be an underground area where bodies were stored but the entrance to it has not yet been found. There is no electricity to the building and if it were saved then there is no obvious use to which the mortuary could be put, other perhaps than as a small exhibition area.

2. Frederick Abberline (died 1929 aged 86) was the detective in charge of investigating the Jack the Ripper murders where at least five and possibly eleven London prostitutes were murdered in 1888. Their throats had been cut and their bodies mutilated. The Ripper was never caught. A book published in 2009 suggested that in fact there never was a Jack the Ripper, that he was invented by journalists in the *Star* newspaper to increase its circulation and that the murders had been carried out by several different people. Abberline was buried in an unmarked grave but a headstone was added in 2007, 78 years after his death, thanks to the work of a group of retired Metropolitan Police officers. (Location Z2/59N).

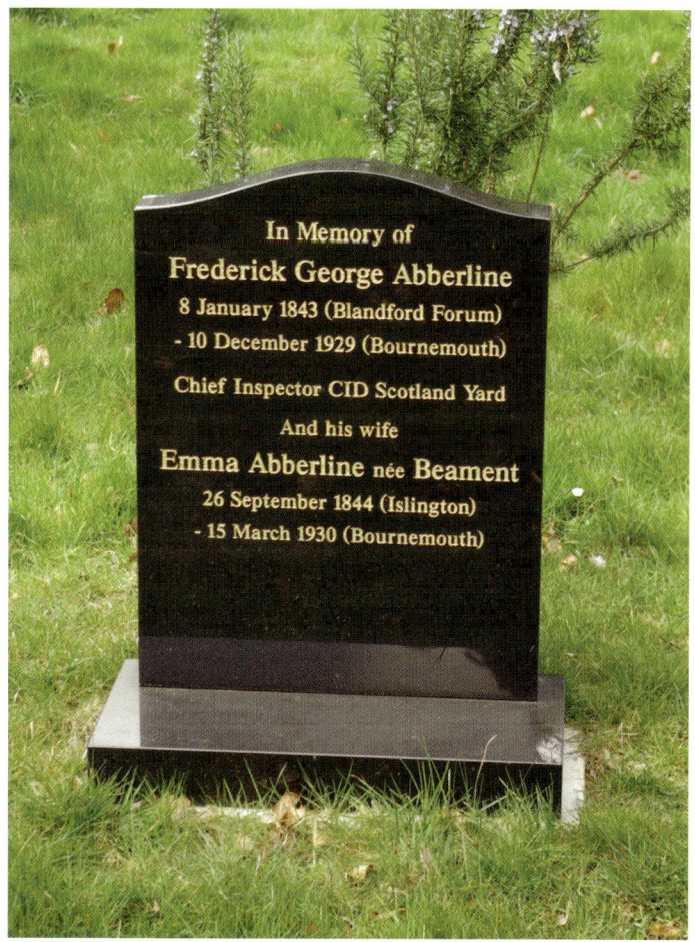

Within the graveyard are the graves of 48 victims from the First World War and 38 from the Second. There are a number of interesting graves of people who have been part of Bournemouth's history. The diagram on the following page should aid visitors in finding the location of the graves; many of the headstones have their location marked on the back.

1. The first burial in the cemetery was that of an 18 month old child, Walter Clifford Barnes, son of a shoemaker, who died on 20 April 1878. The grave has a Celtic Cross headstone. (Location N4/14S)

3. Cheng Woo Gow (died 1893 aged 52) was believed to be the world's tallest man at just under 8 feet and was known as the Gentle Giant. He was born in China and came to Bournemouth in 1890. He appeared in exhibitions and variety shows dressed in his Chinese robes and often accompanied by a three foot high dwarf. He was highly educated, toured the world, spoke six languages and was often the guest of monarchs and politicians. He is said to have died of a broken heart shortly after the death of his wife. At his request, he is buried in an unmarked grave. (Location A6/30S).

4. John Nelson Darby (died 1882 aged 81) started a group devoted to Christian evangelism. The group grew rapidly, so he

started a second group in Plymouth and the movmenent became known as the Plymouth Brethren. The group subsequently split in 1848 into Exclusive Brethren and Open Brethren; the former group are sometimes referred to as Darbyites. In 1854 Darby translated the New Testament into German. (Location Z4/38S).

5. John Foss (died 1910 aged 69) Little is known about him but his grave's headpiece is of interest. It is similar to the type that was employed several hundred years ago when the practice was to hammer two stakes into the ground and put a plank across with the name of the person on it. (Location J3/9N).

6. John Elmes Beale (died 1928 aged 80) is buried, along with his wife who died three years earlier. John opened his first shop in Bournemouth in November 1881 when it was known as Fancy Fair. By 1912 the shop had become significantly larger by purchasing adjacent properties. In 1943 the buildings were destroyed by falling bombs and a new store opened in 1952 when for the first time it sold clothing and hard furnishings. Today the department store is simply known as Beales. John was mayor of Bournemouth in 1902, 1903 and 1904; he was made Freeman of the Borough in 1906, the second

when he flew from Holmsley airfield to St Peter's School in Southbourne. (Location V5/94 & 93S). Close by are the graves of his second son and his son's wife. (Location U5/94S).

7. Christopher Crabb Creeke (died 1886 aged 66), whose statue is in front of the BIC, planned the layout of Bournemouth in the middle to late 19th century. He designed this Wimborne Road cemetery, having previously designed the Poole Cemetery which opened in 1854. He is buried close to the chapel that he designed. (Location C4/5S).

person to receive that honour. He had the distinction of being Bournemouth's first Father Christmas in 1885 when he arrived by train at Bournemouth Station and proceeded by sleigh to his shop, to the adulation of the town's children. His mother had made his costume. He also delivered to individual houses any toys purchased at his shop, which was the first to be connected to the local telephone exchange and had the number Bournemouth 1. Cyril Beale, one of John's sons, was the first Father Christmas in the UK to arrive by air

Columbia. At the age of 56 Rattenbury began an affair with a 27 year old woman. He subsequently invited his new mistress into his house and lived with her on the ground floor, whilst his wife lived upstairs. The Rattenburys divorced in 1925 when he married his mistress, who was already twice divorced. But the anger of the society in Victoria forced Francis and his new wife to flee to England and they settled in Bournemouth. In 1934 his new wife, then 39, took their 17 year old chauffeur as a lover. Later that year the chauffeur bludgeoned Francis to death with a mallet. Both were tried for murder. The chauffeur was found guilty and sentenced to be hanged but was reprieved and released seven years later. Rattenbury's wife was found not guilty, released but then committed suicide a few days later. The trial was a sensation in inter-War England. In 1977 Terence Rattigan wrote a play *Cause Célèbre* based on the affair. Both Francis and his wife were buried in unmarked graves to avoid onlookers. However in summer 2008 a new headstone was provided for Francis's grave by the Canadian Authorities. (Location 13/13S for Francis and 13/10s for his wife).

8. Francis Mawson Rattenbury (died 1935 aged 67) was born in England in 1867 but emigrated to Canada when he was 24. Whilst there he designed the Parliament Building in Victoria, British

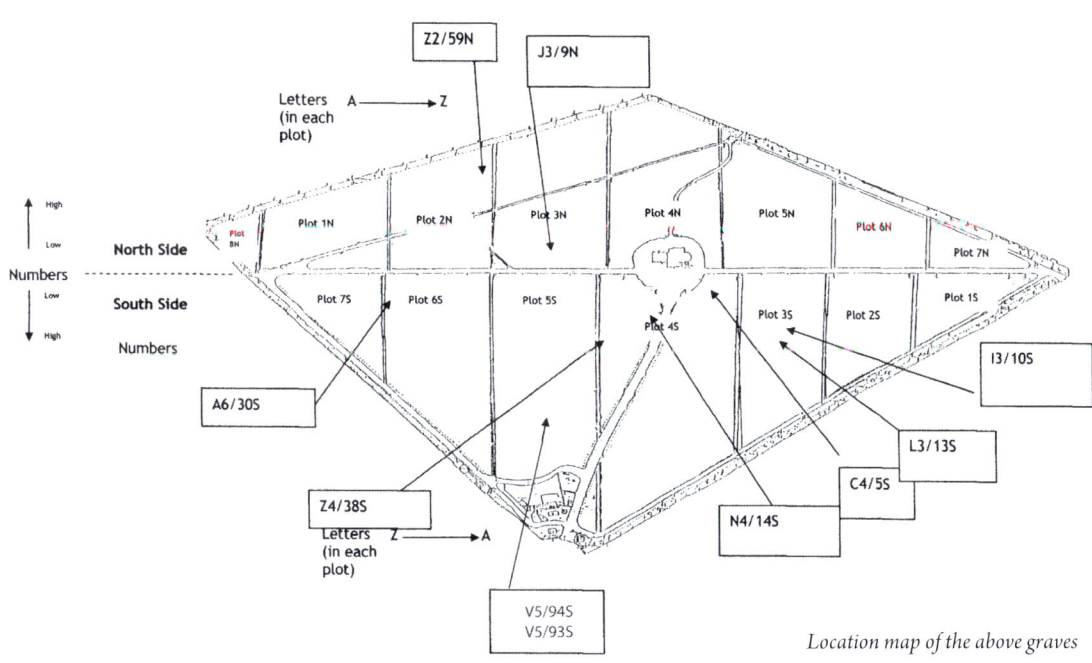

Wimborne Road Cemetery, Wimborne Road, Bournemouth BH3 7AR? Tel: 01202 526238.

At the Richmond Hill Roundabout take the A 347 Wimborne Road. ½ mile further on there is a set of traffic lights. The entrance to the cemetery is directly ahead on the left.

Location map of the above graves

TALBOT VILLAGE

The 1822 Enclosure Act deprived ordinary people of free grazing, timber and game. On inheriting a large sum of money from her father in 1850, Miss Georgina Talbot purchased 300 acres of land and embarked on an experiment. She set out, along with her younger sister Mary Anne, to build 19 cottages, six farms, seven almshouses, a school and a church and to see whether the residents could sustain themselves without help from any charitable source. The farms were all less than 30 acres but the cottages each had exactly one acre of land. All tenants had grazing rights over 150 acres of uncultivated heathland. The area was known as Talbot Village. The cottages were for the working classes and if someone subsequently came into money they had to leave. Above all they had to make their land support themselves and family. No lodgers were allowed and no trade permitted, other than the sale of their produce. The experiment did not go down well with the local landed gentry and the Talbot sisters experienced considerable aggravation but it proved successful. Most of the original Talbot Village has now been sold, sometimes with the Council using compulsory purchase orders. Whites Farm farmhouse remains but all of the other farms and their buildings have now gone.

Georgina Talbot died soon after the village church was completed and the consecration of it had to be brought forward in order that the funeral service and her burial could take place there. She had designed her own memorial and although she died in 1870 the date on her memorial (which is at the rear of the church) looks like 1850. This was thought to be because she died in early January of that year and the stonemason began to put 1869 before realising his mistake and the correction looks more like 1850 than 1870. Walking up the path from Georgina's memorial leads to her sister's memorial where there too is a stonemason's mistake in that it show her sister's name as Marianne rather than Mary Anne.

Commencement of the building of the church was in 1867 and was the last building to be built in the village; no stained glass windows were allowed – the first ones were added in 1920. During its time the church has had only four vicars, although the current vicar is retiring in February 2010. The size of the congregation has increased in recent years to such an extent that a major extension was built in 1986 with the chancel of the old church now used as a small chapel. A new hall was added in 1992. Most of the cost of the build came from the Talbot Village Trust set up by the two sisters. The church's font is believed to be about 2000 years old. It was found in pieces in the River Tiber in Rome by Sir George Talbot.

The almshouses were built in Portland Stone at the same time as the school. There were seven dwellings, intended for the old or infirm. Each resident was expected to help others in time of need.

The first baptism for which it was used was of Emma Georgina Taylor, named after Georgina Talbot; Emma was born on the same day as Georgina died! The carved stone over the porch is of St Mark and came from Bournemouth's first church in **the Square**.

Each cottage had a brick pig sty and a well which collected water drained through the gravel. The residents paid a low rent but had to maintain their cottages themselves.

*The school, built in 1862, used some of the building material from the two cottages which formed Bournemouth's first church in **the Square** and which were demolished in 1838.*

St Mark's Church, Talbot Village, Wallisdown Road, Bournemouth Tel: 01202 529349.

From the cemetery turn right along Wimborne Road. You will first need to turn left and then double back on yourself. At the fourth (University) roundabout turn right into Talbot Village. The church is along the lane to the south of the school.

KINSON CHURCH

St Andrew's Church, Kinson is the oldest church in Bournemouth. It is likely that there was a church on the site during Saxon times. Parts of the present church, notably the tower, date from around 1100 AD although most of the church dates from middle to late 19th century. Many of the early graves in the graveyard are those of smugglers, the most famous being that of Robert Trotman who was killed on the beach near Bournemouth in 1765, whilst smuggling tea. The grave in front of the church was said to be a dummy grave in which smugglers stored their contraband. However the carving on the grave stone states that it contains the bodies of William Oakley and his wife Jane and records show that there was a William Oakley living in the parish at that time. The oldest grave dates from 1667 and is to the west of the church close to the tower. The church is sometimes referred to as the 'Smugglers' Church'

St Andrew's Church, Millhams Road, Kinson. Tel: 01202 570010. Open: Monday – Friday 0900 – 1230.

On leaving Talbot village turn right at University Roundabout. 1¾ miles further turn right at the roundabout onto the A31/A348 to Ringwood. 1½ miles on, at the Bear Cross Roundabout, turn right on to the A341. ¾ mile further on turn left down Trueman Road. Turn left at the end of the road and the church is 100 yards on the left.

STOUR VALLEY WAY

The River Stour rises in Wiltshire although most of the river flows through Dorset. The Stour Valley Way is a designated footpath that runs along most of the river's 65 miles length. There are stretches of the river that are very peaceful as it winds its way to **Tuckton** and **Christchurch.** Two parts that allow easy parking and can be readily reached on the return from Kinson Church to Bournemouth are those at Granby Road and at Throop Mill.

There has been a mill on the Throop Mill site since Saxon times and one is mentioned in the Domesday Book when it was known as Holdenhurst Mill. The present building dates from the 19th century and is Grade II listed. It is in need of renovation. The mill had a diesel engine installed in the 1940s, which was replaced by an electric engine in 1960. The mill ceased operating in 1972 and the building closed in 1981 on the death of the miller, Cecil Biles. The building still contains its milling equipment. The footpath at the side of the mill leads to the weir with its six sluice gates and to open countryside beyond.

To reach the River Stour, rejoin the A341 and turn left. After 1 mile turn right at the roundabout on to the A347. After ½ mile, keep left at the next roundabout. After ¼ mile turn left into Muscliffe Lane and the Granby Road car park is ¼ mile on the left. To reach Throop Mill, turn left on leaving Granby Road car park and continue for ¾ mile along the narrow road. Turn left at the junction. ⅓ mile further on turn left and Throop Mill car park is 100 yards on the left. The footpath and mill are 100 yards further along the road.

HOLDENHURST

Holdenhurst is where Bournemouth had its earliest origins. The Domesday Book of 1068 informs us that Holeest, as Holdenhurst was known, belonged to William the Conqueror and was the centre of a farming community; the grain being taken to Holdenhurst Mill, later known as Throop Mill. The village was given by William's son, Henry I, to the de Redvers family who were relatives and supporters of the king, before it was once more returned to the monarch in 1293 and then to Christchurch Priory until 1808 when it became a separate parish. The parish of Holdenhurst at that time stretched from Christchurch in the east to Poole in the west with most of the land being barren heathland. In 1894 part of the parish was transferred to the new parish of Bournemouth until it was absorbed wholly into Bournemouth in 1931.

Holdenhurst's original church was on what is today known as the 'Consecrated Ground' a few yards from the existing church, along Church Lane. However by 1829 the church had become in such a poor state and too small for the parish of 600 that a new church was built, the land for it being given by Sir G I Tapps whose family's house was at Hinton Admiral (see page 132). The new church, dedicated to St John the Evangelist, was consecrated in 1834 and the old church then demolished. This church (and before it the old church) was Bournemouth's main church until St Peter's opened in 1845 (page 36).

The church's font was originally in the old church and is thought to be of Saxon origin; the remains of the hinges used to lock the cover so that nobody could be baptised during the Interdict period are still visible. The beautiful reredos has tessellations from the Mount of Olives and mosaics from Constantinople and Rome.

Holdenhurst's most famous family was the Dean family. The family were, in the middle of the 17th century, simple farmers but

within 300 years had become millionaires and the richest family in the area after opening a bank. They owned many acres of land in what is now the centre of Bournemouth and later gave much of it to the town, including the Dean Park cricket ground. In 1887 the fortune passed to cousins and the family took the name of Cooper Dean, whose bequests to Bournemouth included Middle Chine and the West Overcliff Drive. By the 1950s the family was extremely rich owning much of Central Bournemouth. However with no heirs the family line ended in 1984 with the death of Edith Cooper Dean, although the name lives on in the charities she and her sister Alice had set up. There is a window in the church given by Edith in memory of her parents on the right as you leave and there are graves to various members of the Dean and Cooper Dean families in the churchyard.

The River Stour can be reached after a short walk alongside the village green and down Sturt Lane. As you leave the village and just before re-joining Throop Road, you pass the Old School and the Vicarage Cottages on the right and the Vicarage and Old Forge on the left.

On leaving the car park at Throop Mill, turn left. After ½ mile turn left into Holdenhurst Village Road. The village and church are ½ mile further on.

WESTBOURNE

Westbourne on the western edge of the Borough, was developed in the second half of the 19th century and was initially planed to have just 60 villas on spacious plots. The area has a village-like feel, with a range of shops and eating places which are mainly family owned. The shopping arcade has Grade II listing; it used to be an orchard owned by the Bournemouth builder Henry Joy. Looking down from high within the arcade are 22 grotesques said to be members of Henry Joy's family! Robert Louis Stevenson moved to the area in 1884, the same year as the arcade was constructed.

Take the Wessex Way to the Boundary Roundabout just inside Poole. The second exit is Seamore Road which leads back into Westbourne.

One of the 22 grotesques.

SKERRYVORE GARDENS

Skerryvore Gardens is a memorial to Robert Louis Stevenson. At the time of writing the novel *Treasure Island*, Robert was in poor health, so his father bought a house in Bournemouth for Robert and his wife to live in. The couple named the house 'Skerryvore' after a Scottish lighthouse built by his father's firm on an isolated rock several miles off the coast of Scotland. Robert took only three days to write *The strange case of Dr Jekyll and Mr Hyde* following a dream. However his wife criticised the story so much that he burnt it and re-wrote it to his wife's satisfaction. The book was published in 1886 in the same year that he wrote *Kidnapped*. Although Robert felt trapped in Bournemouth his wife loved it. Nevertheless shortly after the death of Robert's father, they emigrated to America in 1888 where Robert died of a brain haemorrhage in 1894 at the age of 44. Their house 'Skerryvore' was destroyed by a bomb during the Second World War but the site it occupied is now a memorial garden with a plaque and a model of the Skerryvore lighthouse.

Follow the one-way system through Westbourne and turn right at the traffic lights. R.L. Stevenson Avenue is the second turning on the left. Skerryvore is at the end, opposite across Alum Chine Road.

The model of Skerryvore lighthouse.

ALUM CHINE

Alum Chine obtained its name because of the mining for alum (aluminium oxide) that was carried out there in the middle of the 16th century. The chine is Bournemouth's longest chine and has a tropical 'Treasure Island' themed garden on the cliff side. There is a plant trail through the garden, details of which are displayed on a board, as well as in a leaflet obtained from the Argyll Gardens Bowling Club on West Overcliff Drive to the east of the upper exit of the themed garden. There is a children's play area at the foot of the chine, as well as a new water play area for your children and the popular Vesuvio Bar Restaurant (Tel: 01202 759100).

Turning right on leaving R.L. Stevenson Avenue and then left at the roundabout along Alum Hurst Road leads to the foot of the chine. Turning left on leaving R.L. Stevenson Avenue leads to West Cliff Road and then West Overcliff Drive from which there are entrances to the chine. The entrance closest to Argyll Gardens and from which the Green Flag flies, leads down to the beach via the Tropical Gardens. There is a small café on Argyll Gardens during the summer. The Land Train goes along the promenade from *Pier Approach* and terminates at the foot of Alum Chine.

Halfway up the chine is a suspension bridge. It was from here in 1892 that the 18-year-old Winston Churchill fell while playing with his brother, following which Winston was unconscious for three days.

BOURNEMOUTH NATURAL SCIENCE SOCIETY AND MUSEUM

The Natural Science Society began in 1903 and its offices and collection moved into different locations around the town until 1920. The museum itself dates from this time when the Society acquired its present premises (an 1880 Grade II listed building) for the sum of £2,700. The museum remains in a time-warp and is justifiably proud of it. Many of the specimens date from the 19th century when collecting from the wild was acceptable. Over time such practices have become unacceptable and many similar collections in towns throughout the country have been destroyed. Here you see the collection as it was in the early part of the last century. Almost all of the articles in the museum have been donated by the Society's members over the years, often in the form of entire collections, in many cases built up in the years prior to the establishment of the Society.

It is a wonderful museum and visitors are shown round by its Curator, John Cresswell, with pride and enthusiasm: the Goliath Beetle – the largest beetle in the world; a perfectly formed shell no larger than a pin head; the White's Thrush the first to be seen in the UK in 1828 and immediately shot down; the Passenger Pigeon which were so numerous in America that they blotted out the sun but became extinct in 1914; the pictures of past Presidents of the Society; the diorama rescued when Bournemouth Council closed one of

its museums; the skull collection; the archaeological collection with hand axes dating back over 550,000 years, mainly discovered during the start of the 20th century as Bournemouth underwent a major housing development; the 500-item Egyptian Room, the third largest Egyptian collection in the south-west of England, with the 2,600 year old mummy whose name was Tahema and who is thought to have died at the age of 28; the collection of ushabti figures, which were models of actual people and were buried with the mummified body of the deceased and which were thought to

A full programme of events is arranged throughout the year, with lectures on almost every Tuesday evening and Wednesday and Saturday afternoons.

Bournemouth Natural Science Society, 39 Christchurch Road, Bournemouth BH1 3NS Tel: 01202 553525 Open to the public most Tuesday mornings from 1000-1200 although it is advisable to make an appointment. It is not wheelchair accessible. Free admission, although donations are appreciated.

Drive past the Royal Bath Hotel and go across St Peter's Roundabout (2nd exit). At the Lansdown Roundabout ¼ mile further on take Christchurch Road (4th exit). The museum is a little under ½ mile on the right.

turn back into real people as the nobility passed over to the other side; the butterfly collection consisting of 16 display cabinets which must surely be one of the best collections in the country; the casts of dinosaur footprints, and many more items. There is a separate Mineral Room and a library of over 5,000 books. The rear garden contains a number of exotic trees and shrubs for attracting wild life so as to make a 'living' museum to complement the 'dead' museum inside.

THE KNOLE AND FREEMASONS' MUSEUM

The Knole, which was set in five and a half acres of land, was built by Edmund Christy in 1872 as his home. The building in the late 19th and early 20th centuries was considered to be one of the finest in Bournemouth and is still one of the town's finest Victorian buildings. It is Grade II listed. Christy's wealth was based on the making of hats and towels and the family's felt hat-making empire was the largest in Europe employing more than 3000 workers. Adjacent to the main entrance of The Knole is a plaque depicting the Vision of St Hubert. St Hubert is the patron saint of Furriers and Trappers. Towards the top of the plaque on either side are the initials EC of the owner; on the reverse, inside the building, is the oratory. Edmund Christy left Bournemouth in 1880 and died in Shropshire, 12 years later at the age of 75.

The Knole was sold in 1882 and the building was put to several uses before being bought by Bournemouth Masonic Buildings Ltd in 1956, while most of the gardens were sold for development. The

Knole was significantly enlarged and modified during the next two years. It is now home to 19 lodges, the oldest being the Lodge of Hengist that dates to the middle of the 19th century

The museum is in the basement of The Knole and traces the history of Freemasonry in Bournemouth. The curator, Michael Drayton, introduces you to the world of the Freemasons, to the many jewels (medals) that are on display, to the persecution of Freemasons by the Nazis, to the First World War soldier who

obtained his VC following a ballot, and much more. It is an interesting exhibition and well worth seeing. However it is the tour of The Knole that is likely to be the most interesting. In particular the Meeting Room with four hand-carved chairs, the Banners some more than 100 years old of the 19 lodges and the list of the various Masters. Freemasonry emerged as a secret society at the end of the 17th century although it is possible that it started as long ago as the early 14th century around the Knights Templar. As little as 10 years ago,

such was the secret nature of the society, visitors would not have been shown the building unless they were Freemasons.

Knole Road, from Christchurch Road to The Knole, is a Conservation Area. The properties are mainly of late Victorian origin on spacious plots with those on the elevated east side the most interesting to see.

For further details of The Knole, see 'The Knole – The Story of the Home of Freemasonry in Bournemouth, 1958 – 2008' by Michael Drayton, available from the museum. Much of the information on the Knole and *St Clement's Church* is taken from this source.

Freemasons' Hall, Knole Road, Bournemouth BH1 4DH Tel: 01202 304883 / 393344. Open: Every Tuesday and Thursday from 0930 – 1200 but closed during July and August. Free admission.

From the Bournemouth Natural Science Society & Museum, continue along Christchurch Road for ¼ mile to the traffic lights. Continue across and the first turning on the left is Knole Road. The Knole is 200 yards on the left.

ST CLEMENT'S CHURCH

The parish of St Clement's was established in 1871 and the foundation stone of the church was laid in the same year by the Rev. Morden Bennett, the first vicar of St Peter's. The church is named after Pope St Clement I, who in the 19th century was the patron saint of Felt Hatters. It was designed by John Sedding, a pupil of George Street who had designed **St Peter's Church**. This Victorian Gothic building was opened in 1873 although the tower was added 20 years later. What immediately strikes the visitor on entering is the magnificent stone Rood Screen that separates the nave from the chancel and is the only single stone rood screen in Britain. On top is the Rood or Crucifix. Even more spectacular is the Reredos – ornamental screen covering the wall at the back of the

altar. It was constructed in 1883 and at the time was the largest such piece of work of its kind. The carvings on the beautiful stone pulpit depict the four Apostles Matthew, Mark, Luke and John. The church, like **St Peter's** and **St Stephen's** churches, is Grade I listed. The Parish Hall was once a chapel and has Grade II listing.

The building of St Clements was planned by Edmund Christy and was commence at the time of building his home, The Knole. He also had built two cottages for the curates, a school, an orphanage, a vicarage and a convent for the Sisters of Bethany. The school opened in 1877 and is still there at the rear of the church and is known as St Clement's and St John's Church of England Infants School. The vicarage has been replaced by a modern vicarage and the convent and orphanage have been replaced by the Bethany Church of England Junior School. The two cottages are attached to the infants school, facing St Clement's Road.

St Clement's Church, St Clement's Road, Boscombe, Bournemouth, Dorset BH1 1DZ Tel: 01202 423747. Open: Tuesday 1400 – 1600

On leaving The Knole turn left along Knole Road, and the church is ¼ mile along on the right, on the corner with St Clement's Road.

SPRINGBOURNE

Springbourne has always been closely linked with Boscombe and at one time was known as Boscombe Heath. It derived its name from being the source of a spring which then flowed underground into Boscombe Chine. The spring has long since disappeared.

The Cricketers is Bournemouth's oldest pub. It was built as a coaching house in 1847 and for several years was integral with a brewery. The original stained glass windows are still here. Attached to the pub used to be a boxing gym where Bournemouth's milkman Freddie Mills trained; he was later to become world light-heavy-weight champion. Not much of the original pub remains and so the building does not have listed status. The cricket ground was to the south of the pub and a short walk from St Clement's Church.

Cleveland Road is opposite the north side of St Clement's Church. After crossing the railway bridge, take the first turning on the left, Windham Road and the Cricketers Pub is a few hundred yards along on the right.

BOSCOMBE

On Palmerston Road is the old water tower built in 1875 to contain 160,000 gallons of water 'to give a good supply of water to the people of Boscombe and Springbourne'. It has now been converted into private residences

On leaving St Clement's Church, turn right and then right again into St Clement's Road. The road bears right in Palmerston Road and then direct to the centre of Boscombe.

There are records of Boscombe existing as long ago as the late 13th century but at that time it was mainly a common, covered with gorse. It was originally known as 'Boscumbe', which is an old English word meaning 'valley with spiky plants'. The area began to really develop in the middle of the 19th century, first as three separate areas, namely Boscombe Spa, Boscombe Estate and St Clement's and then, by the end of the 1870s, as one. Boscombe finally merged with Bournemouth in 1876, the two being separated by the chine.

An imposing building in Boscombe is The Royal Arcade, built in 1892. Besides offering an indoor shopping promenade it also provided entertainment from the first floor balcony by a small orchestra or a manual organ – the organ was later removed to the Isle of Wight.

The old water tower.

Above and opposite: The Royal Arcade.

In 1895, three years after the Royal Arcade was built, the Grand Pavilion Theatre opened. Since then it has undergone several name changes, the latest being the O2 Academy Bournemouth. Previously it had been, misleadingly, known as The Opera House. It underwent restoration and refurbishment costing three million pounds in 2007 which restored much of its Victorian splendour, including the two grand Royal Boxes. It is Grade II listed. There used to be cages in the basement for keeping lions and other animals for performances of the circus that were held in the nearby Kings Park. A wide variety of entertainment is held at the O2 Academy and it has won the national award for the best UK Live Entertainment Venue. The gargoyle on the building opposite is a figure of a devil. This was placed there as a protest by the religious people at the time of its opening who objected to the bawdy nature of the theatre opposite. The main shopping area used to be referred to as the 'Golden Mile' but is now a shadow of its former glory.

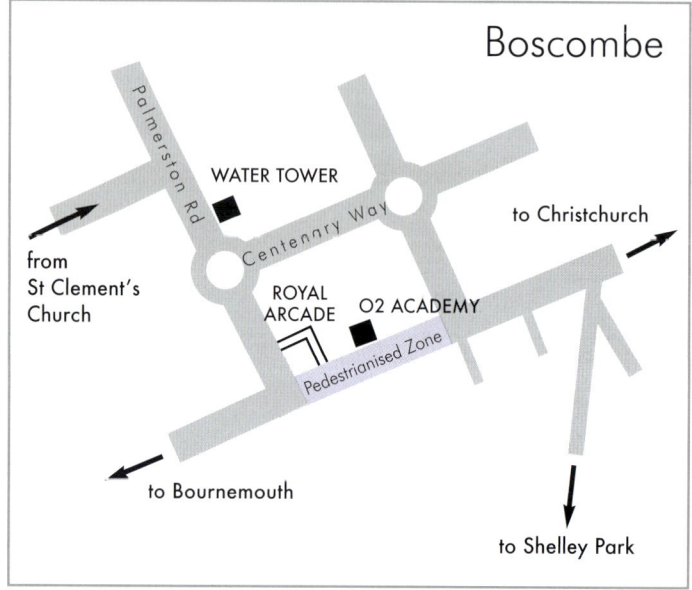

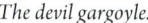

The devil gargoyle.

O2 Academy Bournemouth, 570 Christchurch Road, Boscombe, Bournemouth BH1 4BH. Tel: 01202 399922. Tickets from 08701 989898.

The home ground of AFC Bournemouth (The Cherries) is in Kings Park, to the north of Boscombe, where bowls, athletics and other events take place throughout the year. (AFC Bournemouth, Dean Court, Bournemouth BH7 7AF Tel: 01202 726300).

Boscombe's open air market is held from 0900 – 1700 every Thursday and Saturday all year in the Christchurch Road pedestrianized area.

SHELLEY PARK

In 1801 Boscombe Cottage was built surrounded by 17 acres of land. After several owners it was purchased by Sir Percy Florence Shelley, son of the Romantic poet Percy Bysshe Shelly, for his mother but she died before she could move in. The house was later substantially rebuilt by the Shelley family in 1865 to include a 200 seat theatre, which was enlarged to 300 seats the following year. The name has been changed several times until finally being known as Shelley Manor. Its main use since 1918 was as a school or college but was vacated in 2001. It is now being refurbished as private residential accommodation, together with a medical centre, pharmacy and café. The Grade II listed theatre and some adjoining rooms are being retained for community use. The theatre itself, which seated 220, was planned to have £¼ million spent on it for refurbishment but there is some doubt as to whether the money will be available and at the present time the theatre is not open to the public. There was also a Shelley Museum (known as the 'rooms') but it is not clear who now has the exhibits that were there. Most of the original land is now a park.

Skirting round Boscombe shopping centre leads back to Christchurch Road. Take the second turning on the right (Chessel Avenue) and Shelley Park is ¼ mile on the right.

BOSCOMBE SPA VILLAGE

The Boscombe Spa was a mineral spring emanating from the eastern side of the north of Boscombe Chine. A small summer house was built over it to encourage visitors to the spa and around 1870 it was planned to build a number of marine villas for letting. However the villas were never built, so the planned village of Boscombe Spa did not develop at that time and the spring itself disappeared in the 1920s. In 1874 the Boscombe Spa Hotel was built. Initially it failed and the building was used as a school but in 1885 the hotel reopened and has continued as a hotel since that time. Today the luxury Chine Hotel is set in three acres of mature gardens with direct access to the beach. There is a hall of fame on its lower-ground floor with photos of some of the many stars who have stayed there over the years.

Chine Hotel, 19-25 Boscombe Spa Road, Bournemouth BH5 1AX. Tel: 01202 396234.

The Chine Hotel.

In 2008 Bournemouth Council sold a car park in the area and invested £11 million pounds from the sale to regenerate the Boscombe Spa area, which had had little spent on it since the 1950s. The Boscombe Overstrand Building has been refurbished and now incorporates 59 purpose built beach huts. Their interiors have been individually and professionally designed by a local artist and are thought to be the best beach huts in the world! All have mains electricity and some have running hot and cold water, French doors, balconies and bespoke furniture. There is a penthouse, doubles and singles. 31 of the huts are being sold on 25-year leases costing from £65,000 for singles to £90,000 for doubles; the remainder will be hired out. They are being called 'beach pods' and will be for day use only. In addition there is a glass fronted restaurant, a surf-themed shop, a marine surf academy, public changing rooms, toilets and hot showers, a Council office and an RNLI office. The Council is now planning to introduce a few beach huts specifically designed and built for the disabled.

The Grade II listed Boscombe Pier was built in 1889 by a private company and sold to Bournemouth Council in 1903. The pier head was added in 1926. As in Bournemouth, part of the pier was demolished during the war for fear of a German invasion and by 1950 it was practically a wreck. The pier was refurbished between 1958 and 1960 but closed in 1988 on safety grounds. It was again refurbished in 2008 when the Mermaid Theatre, the restaurant and the indoor skating rink were replaced by a viewing platform. The listed entrance building now includes a café and shop.

The 5.5 metre high granite sculptures on the pier approach roundabout were erected in October 2008. The two massive blocks, hewn from a single piece of granite, cost £70,000 and were shipped from China. The two halves depict the sun and moon rising and falling in the east and west. The highly polished surfaces, which have an anti-graffiti coating, reflect the light from the sea and sky.

The Boscombe Overstrand Building.

The listed entrance to Boscombe Pier.

Granite sculptures near Boscombe Pier.

The artificial reef.

From Shelley Park, continue to the end of Chessel Avenue and turn right. At the following T-junction turn left and at the next T-junction turn left again which leads to the pier. During the summer there is free bus travel between the beach and Boscombe town centre if you use the Hawkwood Road car park, or arrive by train at Pokesdown Station. (The No 11 Bus between 1005 and 1900). The Land Train travels every 20 minutes between the Boscombe and Bournemouth piers, along the promenade seafront. For the Chine Hotel, take the second turning on the left as you leave Pier Approach.

Europe's first artificial surf reef, and the fourth in the world, was 10 years in the planning and was completed in 2010. It consists of 55 bags filled with sand and then laid on the sea bed one-by-one. The reef, which is 225 meters from the beach, then acts as a ramp, pushing the waves upward and doubling their size; it does not produce waves but amplifies existing waves. It cost nearly £3 million pounds to construct and is sometimes referred to as 'Weight's Reef' after the man who first proposed it in 1993. Its critics say that it does not work, was over budget, is too small and is not safe. It is certainly true that it was over budget and the sale of the surf pods which was to pay for it was slow, with only seven being sold in the first six months. However the number of good surfing days is expected to double since the reef was built and unquestionably it has helped in the regeneration of the area. Time will tell whether indeed it is Boscombe's Folly. Other water sports on offer in the area include kite-surfing, windsurfing, wakeboarding, kayaking, scuba-diving and skimboarding. The South Coast Surfing Championships are held in Boscombe every three years.

Sand used for the building of the surf reef.

BOSCOMBE CHINE GARDENS

Boscombe Chine Gardens were first laid out during the latter part of the 19th century but fell into decline during the 20th century. However with the help of a Heritage Lottery Fund grant the Chine gardens have been restored to their original Victorian splendour and the area is now officially recognised as a nature reserve. There is a multi-use games area, a water-play area, mini-golf and a terrace café in the gardens. The Land Train starts from here and travels to Bournemouth Pier.

Café and 18 hole mini-golf are open from 1000 – 1800 during summer and 1000 – 1600 in winter.

There is an entrance to the chine from Boscombe Pier approach. The entrance to the top of the gardens is opposite Knole Road.

SOUTHBOURNE AND FISHERMAN'S WALK

Southbourne dates from 1870 when 230 acres of land, including a 1 mile sea frontage, was purchased by Dr Compton and Southbourne on Sea was created. To ease access to the area he constructed Belle Vue Road and *Tuckton* Bridge. The population in the area grew steadily over the next few years and the town's first permanent church, St Katharine's, was built in 1883. The stained glass windows are a feature of the church. It was planned that the town would rival Bournemouth but in fact it became part of Bournemouth in 1901

St Katharine's Church, Church Road, Southbourne, BH6 4AR. Tel: 01202 420571. Open: 0900 – 1300 (enquire at the church office).

Fisherman's Walk is the path that leads to the cliff top and beach from Southbourne's shopping area with its entrance directly opposite the bus stop. The narrow straight path down the side of Fisherman's Walk was originally the boundary of a large estate that was sold in 1893. At the time the estate was sold, the area to the west of the path, was widened to its current width. The gardens were created in 1913 and named after the path, which was used by local fishermen on their way to the beach. The bandstand at the heart of the gardens is still there. Some of the original pine trees still exist, whilst others have been replaced with trees such as horse chestnuts.

The rose gardens (or 'Rest Gardens' as they were known) and pond toward the south entrance were added in the 1920s when there were many more

St Katharine's Church.

Sculpture trail.

pine trees. Thanks to the award of a lottery grant in 2007 a number of bat and bird boxes have been fixed in the trees, as well as a trail of wooden sculptures. These images have been carved by a local artist in oak taken from Queens Park. They depict species than can be found in Fisherman's Walk, such as frogs, bats, hedgehogs, oak leaves, toadstools and butterflies.

At the southern end of Fisherman's Walk is the Commodore Hotel to the east and the Riva Café directly opposite, while to the west are crazy golf and putting greens, as well as a small children's play area. Beyond the café is one of Bournemouth's many zigzag paths leading to the beach, as well as a cliff lift that operates during summer months. This one of the few places where dogs are allowed on the beach all year round.

The Riva Café is open 0830 – 1800 in winter and 0830 – 2300 in summer. Tel: 01202 422002.

From Boscombe continue along Christchurch Road for ½ mile to the traffic lights. Turn right (B3059) signposted South-bourne and Tuckton. The entrance to Fisherman's Walk is just under ½ mile on the right. For St Katharine's Church, continue past Fisherman's Walk for a further mile along Southbourne Road and Belle Vue Road. Church Road is on the right and St Katharine's Church is 100 yards along on the right.

TUCKTON

The upper limit of the River Stour, as far as navigation by boats is concerned, is Tuckton Bridge which spans the River Stour. The bridge is over 100 years old and is one of the earliest reinforced concrete structures in the UK and for this reason has listed status. On the up-river side of the bridge is a Harvester Pub with a pleasant garden overlooking the river. The footpath on this part of the river can be reached by crossing the bridge and taking the first turning on the left. A car parking area is signposted and the path continues from there. A short distance downstream from the bridge is the Tuckton Tea Gardens, with a small golf course and putting green. There are good views from the garden across the river.

The café serves light lunches and runs barbeque cruises on a Saturday evening during the summer; this is a two hours cruise on the river followed by the barbeque at the café.

The Vintage Ferry Service starts from the grounds of the Tea Gardens and goes to Wick Ferry, Christchurch Quay and **Mudeford Sandbanks**, taking about 40 minutes to cruise down the River Stour. The boats, which were built in 1934 and 1935, have been specially designed to cope with the shallowness of the river. The propeller system is located in a tunnel beneath the boat which draws water up and then pushes it out at the stern. Self drive motor boats taking up to eight passengers can also be hired, as can rowing boats with a maximum of four people. A recent addition are Bumper Boats for children to play in.

A pleasant walk down the riverside path leads to one of the entrances to the **Hengistbury Head** Nature Reserve.

Tuckton Tea Gardens, 323 Belle Vue Road, Southbourne, Bournemouth BH6 3BA Tel: 01202 429119 – the same number for ferry services and boat hire. Open daily from 0900 to 0430, later in summer, all year other than January.

From St Katharine's Church return to Belle Vue Road and turn right. ½ mile further on is a roundabout. Turn right and the Tea Gardens are immediately on your left. The car park and toilets are a further ¼ mile on the left.

HENGISTBURY HEAD
*See also Christchurch – **Mudeford Sandbank***

The promontory was originally known as Hynesbury Head but was later renamed Hengistbury Head as it is reputed to have been the landing place of Hengist the Jute. It is thought to have been the first urban settlement in the UK, dating from around 10,000 BC. However long before this and probably dating back over 100,000 years there had been nomads in the area. This was when Hengistbury Head would have been on the mouth of the River Solent and Britain was still joined to mainland Europe. During the Bronze Age from 1000 BC the town grew in importance until it reached its peak around 700 BC when it was occupied by the Celts and Britain had become an island. There are several Bronze Age Round Barrows (burial mounds) in the area. At this time it would have been the largest port in the UK, not least because of the high concentration of iron ore in the region which would have been traded on the continent in return for, among other things, Italian wine. The town started to decline during the Roman occupation and was completely abandoned around 450 AD. In the middle of the 19th century a substantial amount of iron ore was extracted from the base of the headland and resulted in the loss of a significant part of the head, mainly by erosion after the end of the quarrying. It was purchased by Bournemouth Council in 1930. The site is of international importance and is officially classified as an Ancient Monument.

The area is a major tourist attraction with over one million visitors a year, many of whom use the Land Train which leaves from the Hengistbury Head, Hiker Café, taking about 10 minutes for the 1½ miles drive to the terminus at **Mudeford Sandbank/Mudeford Spit** which, although technically in Bournemouth comes under the control of Christchurch. During wet weather when there are few tourists, the train is replaced by a four-wheeled drive vehicle. Close to the Hiker Café are a number of expla-

Mudeford Spit, with Mudeford Harbour in the foreground and Hengistbury Head in the background.

nation boards giving details of the Nature Reserve, the wildlife that can be seen and a brief history of the region at the time of the Iron and Stone Ages.

From the roundabout in front of the café is a footpath going north which leads to the Hengistbury Head Outdoor Centre, which is run by Brockenhurst College. From here there are excellent views across

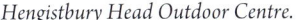

Hengistbury Head Outdoor Centre.

The Land Train.

the harbour. It is at this point that a breach is likely to occur if erosion continues which will make Hengistbury Head an island.

Double Dykes.

Iron Age defences.

Hut in the bird sanctuary.

BIRD SANCTUARY

The public are requested not to enter this area and to report to the Ranger the presence of persons in the sanctuary.

There are numbered posts along the route to the Spit and guide books are available for purchase from the Land Train office. As the train departs, it passes through Double Dykes which were two earth ramps separated by a ditch that acted as a defence from attack from the west for the iron age settlers. Although the ramps are not apparent from the main footpath, they are when viewed from a few hundred yards to the west of the Hikers Café. An information board depicts the area's defences as they might have been in the iron age.

The thatched barn near the entrance of the reserve is used as an educational centre. An almost £1 million investment is planned to renovate it and open it to the public which will include a display of items that have been lent to the National History Museum, the British Museum and Oxford University.

The derelict hut a short way further on in the bird sanctuary was used by two rangers who looked after the reserve. A tree growing through the middle of the hut is clearly visible.

Turning right at Post 24 leads to the Quarry and Lily Ponds where iron stone was quarried in the 19th century. Continuing leads to a now deserted coast-guard lookout from where there are excellent views across the harbour to Christchurch and Mudeford.

Returning to Post 24 and continuing along the main path brings you to the Spit which was leased to Christchurch many years ago. Walking back along the cliff face the sand martins' tunnelled nests can be seen in the south facing soft cliffs.

Most of the area is now wheelchair accessible. There is ample car parking space near the Hiker Café which is open from Monday to Friday from 0900 – 1700 and on Saturday and Sundays from 0900 – 1730.

From Tuckton, turn left at the roundabout and rejoin Belle Vue Road. After 200 yards turn left. After a further ¾ mile bear left and the car park is ½ mile further on. The Land Train leaves from outside the Hiker Café, departing every half hour, on the hour (every fifteen minutes in the peak season). The first train leaves at 1000 and the last at 1700. The train returns every half hour at 15 minutes past the hour. Ferries leave from **Mudeford** Quay to **Mudeford Sandbank**.

LV STREETWISE

Streetwise is a life-sized village, constructed inside a 10,000 square foot warehouse. In the village are a high street with shops and office fronts, a two-storey house, garden, park, alleyway, electricity sub-station, railway line, farmyard, heathland, beach and a building site. This award winning attraction is an interactive safety centre whose aim is to raise the awareness of safety in everyday life. A tour takes around two hours and visitors learn how to recognise potential dangers and minimise the associated risks, visiting each area in the village. The centre cost £0.5 million to construct and was opened to the first paying visitor in January 2001. It now costs £0.25 million a year to run and is aimed primarily at school children. Tourists can however visit if they phone beforehand to make an appointment.

One of the highlights, judging by the look on the children's faces, is the mock up of the Virgin Train driver's cab. The simulation drive goes from Bournemouth to Brockenhurst and allows various options to show how easy it is to get killed on railway tracks. Children have the opportunity to drive and stop the train, with the loud squeal of the train's brakes.

Another highlight is the fire in the house where visitors must get down on the floor to escape the smoke and then dial 999. The call is answered by workers in the office.

The latest addition to the collection is half a bus to teach children safety and responsibility on public transport.

A section on internet safety is being developed since one of the greatest dangers to young people today is probably from paedophiles on the internet.

LV Streetwise is a registered attraction with insurance company

LV= the main sponsor. Pre-booking is essential. The centre is well worth a visit in terms of educating the young in all aspects of safety, while at the same time being enjoyable.

Streetwise, Unit 1, Roundways, Elliott Road, Bournemouth, Dorset BH11 8JJ. Tel: 01202 591330. Open: All year, weekdays only 0900 – 1700.

At the Richmond Hill Roundabout on the Wessex Way, take the A347 Wimborne Road. ½ mile further on at the traffic lights turn left and keep straight on (A347 then A3049). At the sixth roundabout turn right (A348) and then at the next roundabout do a 360° turn. Take the first turning on the left which leads into Elliott Road. This is in the same direction as **Talbot Village** and **Kinson** Church.

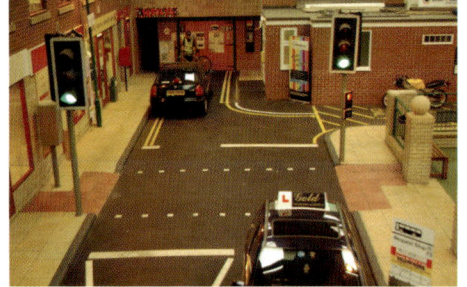

LITTLEDOWN PARK

Littledown Park is 47 acres of landscaped grounds in the north-west of the Borough, close to the out of town Castle-point Shopping Centre, the Royal Bournemouth Hospital and the Crown and County Courts. The park has a children's play area, a large wildfowl lake, a youth centre and a leisure complex, known as the Littledown Centre. In the north of the park is a Miniature Railway run by the Bournemouth & District Society of Model Engineers. The track is ⅓ mile long and passes beneath tress for most of its journey. It can accept locomotives built to 3.5", 5" and 7.25" gauges.

The miniature railway operating times are from 1100 – 1600 on Sundays and Wednesdays.

The Littledown Centre opened in March 1989 and in 2008 was voted by Quest, the UK quality scheme for Sport and Leisure, as the best sports complex in the UK out of 900 similar facilities. It did even better in 2009 when they awarded it the highest possible marks in all categories! It offers a wide range of indoor and outdoor leisure facilities and is one of the largest leisure centres in the country. Its facilities include football & cricket pitches, two swimming pools, waterslides, spa, gym and pools dedicated for toddlers and youngsters. There is a café, bar and free car-parking facilities.

Littledown Centre, Chaseside, Castle Lane East, Bournemouth BH7 7DX. Tel: 01202 417600. Open daily from 0630 – 2200.

Join the Wessex Way going north and leave at the junction signposted for the Hospital (A3060). Turn right at the Cooper Deane roundabout (third exit) for Christchurch. At the traffic lights turn right and the entrance is the right turning at the roundabout.

SPORTING FACILITIES

Bournemouth is a sporting paradise with most kinds of sporting facilities available within Bournemouth or nearby Poole. The two towns co-operate in the provision of many council owned facilities such as **football**, **cricket** and **rugby**. The award-winning, Council-owned Littledown Centre, mentioned above, is the main provider of indoor facilities. For **water sports** it is probably best to go to neighbouring Poole. Whilst Bournemouth waits for its new Olympic-size Ice Stadium at Kings Park complete with curling facilities and building due to start in 2011, **ice skating** can be enjoyed at the Bournemouth International Centre during certain times in winter and summer.

The Borough has some of the best **golf** courses in the south of England; all are 18 holes. Almost in the centre of town is the 18 hole golf course 'The Club' at Meyrick Park (Tel: 01202 786040) which was established in 1894 and is set in 120 acres of parkland. The Solent Meads course at Hengistbury Head has lovely views over Christchurch Harbour to the Priory and Mudeford (Tel: 01202).

The Sir David English Centre is home of the Hub Club, which aims to unite all the local sporting clubs and facilities. Contact the Hub Club Coordinator (Tel: 01202 437809) for details of such sports as **badminton, basketball, BMX, bowls (including indoor bowls), bowling, cheerleading, croquet, fencing, football, gymnastics, ladies kick boxing, horse riding, martial arts, netball, skate-boarding, table-tennis, tennis, trampoline, triathlon and volleyball**. Many sports have classes specifically aimed at the younger person.

What better way is there to keep fit and enjoy yourself than to go **dancing**. Bournemouth is attempting to become the dancing capital of the South and it may already have achieved this. Whatever form of dancing you want, be it ballet, tango, salsa, jive, line or the good old waltz, it will be available somewhere.

The Tourist Information Centre (Tel: 0845 0511700) will inform you where and when your chosen sport is happening.

NIGHT LIFE

Bournemouth has entertainment to meet most tastes. For those who want a traditional form of evening entertainment there are three major show venues, namely the **Pavilion** (see page 34), the **Bournemouth International Centre** (see page 12) and the **Pier Theatre** (see page 9). There is also **The Lighthouse** in Poole (opposite the Poole bus terminus – Tel: 0844 406 8666). Bournemouth's two **cinemas,** the Odeon and the ABC (Tel. for both cinemas: 0871 2244007) are in Westover Road. Several hotels mount their own evening entertainment which can be combined with a meal. The **Village Hotel**, opposite Bournemouth Hospital, about three miles from the centre of Bournemouth, occasionally offer **dinners and show** (Tel: 0870 112 8120). There are a number of **traditional pubs** in the centre of Bournemouth, for example the **Moon in the Square** (4-8 Exeter Road Tel: 01202 652090) which is often full, especially on summer weekends. Another, opposite St Peter's Church, is **The Mary Shelley** (64-67 The Quadrant Centre, St Peter's Road, BH1 2AD) where there are paintings dedicated to the author.

For those with a more varied taste, Bournemouth has scores of bars and nightclubs, some not opening until late in the evening; the town is said to be the clubbing capital of the South. The resort's Town Watch organisation has worked with the clubs to agree a voluntary code of conduct to eliminate any rowdiness and this is assisted by there being a strong police presence at weekends. So although the town is often crowded during a summer weekend, it is also safe. The first winner of the 'Best Bar None' awards, which promotes high standards in the licensed trade, was **Bar So/1812** based in the Royal Exeter Hotel in Exeter Road. (Tel: 01202 438000). It is named after the year in which Tregonwell's villa (now the hotel) was built. A short way further along, at 19 Exeter Road, is **60 Million Post Cards** (Tel: 01202 292697) which has a good outside area for enjoying a drink with friends on a warm evening.

For something different, there is the **Camel Bar** (174 Old Christchurch Road. Tel: 01202 291420). This is an Egyptian-style smoking bar where you can smoke a **hubble-bubble**, watch others do it, or watch the club's **belly-dancer**. The indoor smoking ban applies to hubble-bubble smoking so this takes place in their Camel Garden, which is an outdoor courtyard.

The **O2 Academy Bournemouth** in Boscombe (see page 84) offers a wide range of top quality evening entertainment.

The Poole Hill, Commercial Road and Avenue area on the West Cliff, which is usually referred to as the Triangle, has a number of bars and clubs for the **Gay community**. The area is abuzz on most summer evenings. The multicolour flags outside the buildings identifies them as catering for the Gay community.

'Bournemouth's Bus 'N' Bar Tour', or the **'Party on a Bus'**, as it likes to be known, operates on Saturdays, all year round. They have been operating for seven years and on a busy summer Saturday can have up to 100 passengers on two buses. The buses are double-deckers fitted with flashing lights and a sound system. The tour begins at around 1900 and visits four mainstream bars and clubs, spending about an hour in each. After finishing at the fourth bar passengers are taken to one of the top night clubs. All ages and group sizes (including singles) are catered for. (Tel: 01202 233952).

Bournemouth has three **lap-dancing** clubs in the town centre. Although prices vary between clubs, the entry fee often depends on the time of entry and how busy it is and it is quite likely that on a quiet weekday there is no entry fee. Two of the clubs are in the main night club areas of Old Christchurch Road, namely **For Your Eyes Only** (fyeo) (136 Old Christchurch Road, Tel: 01202 311108) and, almost opposite, **Wiggle** (159 Old Christchurch Road, Tel: 01202 292032) Another is the **Spearmint Rhino Gentleman's Club** (1 Yelverton Road. Tel: 01202 295300) which claims to be the South Coast's No 1 Gentleman's Club and recently had a £1.4 million refit.

The **Adonis Cabaret Show** (Fir Vale Road Tel: 01273 417787) is at the **Lava Ignite** every Saturday from February to November. This **male strip** show started in Vienna in 1996 and has gone from strength to strength since. Tickets must be purchased before the day of the show and there is a minimum group size of four. This is a comedy show intended to give fun and includes comedians and games. The **Lava Ignite** also hosts the **Jaggers Comedy Club** every Saturday for the over 18s, from February to November with top artistes appearing. Pre-booking is advisable, especially during the summer season.

A place not to be missed if there is a show is **Rubyz** (see page 25) and its owner Miss Kitty (real name David Mitchell). The show is great fun but is not for those who may be distressed by sexual innuendo. 80% of the patrons are women. (Tel: 01202 552553).

Every Friday evening, other than during the summer season, the **Centre Stage** hosts the **Funnybone Comedy Club**. Here you can listen to top comedians while enjoying a meal. Centre Stage (next to the Pig and Whistle Pub), 14 Queens Road, Bournemouth BH2 6BE is about a mile from the centre of Bournemouth. (Tel: 01202 540065).

Also at the Centre Stage is the Bournemouth Modern Jazz Club which plays modern **jazz** once a month (Tel: 07811 369062). **Klute** (20 Exeter Road Tel: 01202 252511) offers jazz on the first Tuesday of each month when pre-show dinners are available. The **Miramar Hotel** (East Overcliff Drive Tel: 01202 556581) offers laid back jazz every Sunday evening from 2000, together with dancing. The **Westbeach Restaurant** (Pier Approach Tel: 01202 587785) offers jazz from 2000 every first Thursday of the month. **The Durley Dean Hotel** (Tel: 01202 557711) offers traditional jazz every Monday evening starting at 1900.

The **Royal Wessex Hotel** (see page 12; Tel: 01201 203060) has jazz-based entertainment on Friday and Saturday evenings, between 2200 and 2400, and at Sunday lunch times between 1300 and 1500.

Champions (51 Norwich Avenue West, BH2 6AJ Tel: 01202 757000) is a 200 capacity venue that hosts a variety of events with national and international performers. There are usually four bands, each night playing **rock music**. The admissions price depends on the artistes. There is live music upstairs and a night club on the lower floor. (Closed on Wednesdays). Every Monday evening is **Blues night**, arranged by the Bournemouth Blues Club, with Blues Jam on the first and last Monday of each month.

There are two **casinos,** admission is free and membership is available at the door. Maxims Casino (9 Yelverton Road: Tel: 01202 293188) is open from 1200 – 0500 daily. Mah Jong is played every second Monday of the month. Gala Casino (48 Westover Road: Tel: 01202 553790) opens daily from 1000 – 0500 and new members are made welcome with a free drink and given a £10 bet.

To obtain up-to-the-minute information visit the Tourist Information Centre (Tel: 0845 0511700) on Westover Road for a copy of 'What's On'.

CHRISTCHURCH

Christchurch has two rivers flowing through it, namely the Avon and the Stour, with the shallow Christchurch Harbour being formed by their junction. The original (Saxon) name of Christchurch was 'Twboxneam' or 'Twynham' which are old English words meaning 'between the waters' and is first mentioned in relation to the death of King Alfred in 899 when the burgh (or fort) was seized by the son of King Ethelwold I. The burgh had been built on the orders of King Alfred as a defence against attacks from Viking pirates. William I had a motte-and-bailey castle built about 1074 to enforce his New Forest laws. The town was granted its first parliamentary seat in 1307, which was the last year of the reign of Edward I. However as no one applied for the seat no further writ was granted until 1571. The Parliamentarians captured the town in 1644. It received its charter of incorporation in 1886.

Christchurch sandwiched between the Rivers Stour (on the left) and Avon (on the right).

In 1843 the parish of Christchurch covered an area of nearly 25,000 acres; today it covers just over 1,000 acres, of which nearly 150 acres are water. In the meantime, Bournemouth, Hengistbury Head, Southbourne and Pokesdown, which were once in the parish of Christchurch, have been transferred to the new Borough of Bournemouth. Christchurch is now one of the smallest local authorities in the country with a population of around 46,000.

An open-air market has been held on Mondays since before the year 1150 in the High Street from 0900 to 1600. A Country Fayre is held on Thursdays and the Dorset Farmer's Market on the first Friday morning of each month. The town offers an interesting and enjoyable day out.

From Bournemouth take the Wessex Way north and then the A35 signposted Lyndhurst / Christchurch. The road becomes a dual carriage way at the Bailey Roundabout, just before entering Christchurch. Follow the signs to 'Town Centre' and 'B3059'. ½ mile further on is a large, double roundabout. Follow it round, doing a 180° turn at the Fountain Roundabout. Take the first turning on the left and drive along High Street. At the mini-roundabout go straight ahead (second exit). After 100 yards the road bears sharp right. Another 100 yards further on turn left in front of the **Red House Museum** into Quay Road. There is a car park directly ahead.

PLACE MILL AND QUAY

This Anglo-Saxon water mill is mentioned in the Domesday Book. It operated by using the rise and fall of the tides, augmented by the mill stream diverted from the River Avon. It was used to ground corn until 1908 when it had to close due to structural defects. The building was then used as a boat shed until purchased and restored by Christchurch Council. It now houses a collection of milling artefacts, smuggling memorabilia and archaeology exhibits. There is a gift shop on the ground floor and an art gallery of work by local artists on the first floor.

The Quay, which was used to import stone and coal and export beer and grain, is now used solely by pleasure crafts. Ferries leave the Quay for **Mudeford Sandbanks** or up the River Stour to Wick and **Tuckton.**

MILLENNIUM TRAIL

Mentioned in the Domesday Survey of 1086 valued at 30s a year, being the property of the Canons of the Holy Trinity Church, **PLACE MILL** has medieval stonework and Tudor and 18th century brickwork, and was used for both fulling (cleaning and thickening cloth) and corn grinding until 1908

CHRISTCHURCH LOCAL HISTORY SOCIETY

Place Mill, The Quay, Christchurch, Dorset, BH23 1BY. Tel: 01202 487626. Open: April to September, Tuesday – Sunday 1100 – 1730 (closed 1300 – 1400). Free Admission.

Leaving the Priory car park by the back entrance leads direct to the Quay with Place Mill on the right.

CHRISTCHURCH CASTLE

Christchurch's original motte-and-bailey castle is thought to have been built toward the end of the 11th century. (The 'motte' is the man-made hill which initially would have been crowned with a wooden tower known as the 'keep'; the 'bailey' is the large, flat section of the castle below the keep where buildings were located. The whole would have been enclosed by a wooded fence.) The wooden keep was used by King Stephen in his war with Empress Matilda. It was replaced by a three-storey-high stone keep around

1300. The stone keep fell into disuse in the 14th century but was later involved in the civil war when it was used by the Royalists. It was captured by the Parliamentarians following a siege in 1645 and at the end of the Civil War Cromwell ordered the castle to be demolished leaving it in its present state. The arched remains of the keep show the massive nine foot thickness of the walls.

It is the Constable's Hall in the north-east corner of the bailey, on the bank of the mill stream, that is of most historical significance. This was the living quarters for the occupants of the castle. It dates from around 1160, which was before the building of the stone keep. On the east wall of the Hall, between the two windows, was where the fireplace used to be and the original cylindrical chimney can still be seen towering above the walls. There are only five surviving Norman chimneys in England and this is the only one still attached to its house.

Continuing along the path to the east of the keep and turning left after passing through the gates, brings you to the re-sited Mausoleum of a Mrs Perkins who had a horror of being buried alive.

The area is not fenced off and there is no attendant, so it is open every day, throughout the year.

Leaving Place Mill, cross the bridge over the tributary of the Avon River to the north of the mill and go along Convent Walk behind the Priory Church. At Castle Road, turn left and the entrance to the castle is 100 yards on the left.

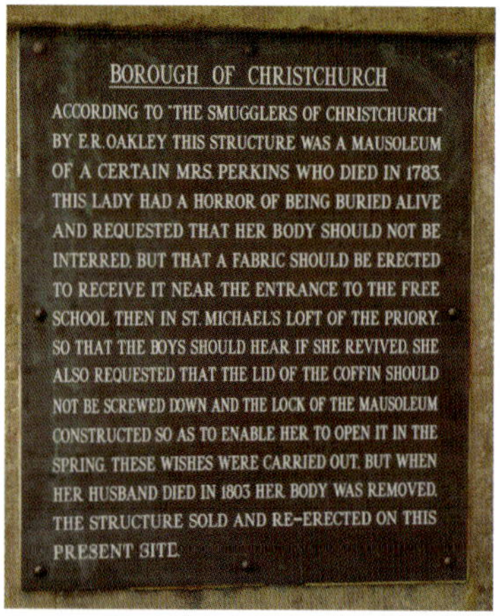

BOROUGH OF CHRISTCHURCH
ACCORDING TO "THE SMUGGLERS OF CHRISTCHURCH" BY E.R. OAKLEY THIS STRUCTURE WAS A MAUSOLEUM OF A CERTAIN MRS. PERKINS WHO DIED IN 1783. THIS LADY HAD A HORROR OF BEING BURIED ALIVE AND REQUESTED THAT HER BODY SHOULD NOT BE INTERRED, BUT THAT A FABRIC SHOULD BE ERECTED TO RECEIVE IT NEAR THE ENTRANCE TO THE FREE SCHOOL THEN IN ST. MICHAEL'S LOFT OF THE PRIORY, SO THAT THE BOYS SHOULD HEAR IF SHE REVIVED. SHE ALSO REQUESTED THAT THE LID OF THE COFFIN SHOULD NOT BE SCREWED DOWN AND THE LOCK OF THE MAUSOLEUM CONSTRUCTED SO AS TO ENABLE HER TO OPEN IT IN THE SPRING. THESE WISHES WERE CARRIED OUT, BUT WHEN HER HUSBAND DIED IN 1803 HER BODY WAS REMOVED, THE STRUCTURE SOLD AND RE-ERECTED ON THIS PRESENT SITE.

YE OLDE GEORGE INN

Ye Olde George Inn is the oldest inn in Christchurch, dating back more than 600 years, although most of it was rebuilt in 1646 after the Civil War. It was initially known as 'The St George and Dragon' but over time became 'The George' and was mistakenly given its present name, after the Hanoverian King, whose picture is displayed on the sign outside. Its history, as a coaching inn, includes the stabling of the horses of the young Princess Victoria before she became queen and the hiding

of contraband by smugglers. There are also claims that priests were hidden in the roof during the Civil War and that prisoners were held in the cellars prior to deportation, although this is disputed. The inn has its own brew, known as YOGI (Ye Olde George Inn) and sells Piddle – a local brew!

Ye Olde George Inn, 2a Castle Street, Christchurch, Dorset, BH23 1DT Tel: 01202 479383.

The inn is 200 yards further along Castle Road after leaving the castle.

CUCKING STOOL

There is a replica cucking stool beside the Mill Stream. During the 15th – 18th centuries stools such as this would have been used to deliver punishment by plunging miscreants into the Mill Stream. Such stools were mainly used on women, in particularly on nagging wives – men were placed in the stocks. The word 'cucking' derives its name from old English words meaning 'faeces' and 'to defecate'. Sometimes the seat would incorporate a chamber pot and the woman fastened to it with her bottom bare. The aim was to humiliate. Their use was only removed from the statute book in 1967. The stools were later also known as 'ducking' stools and, for fear of the effects of graffiti writers, the lane leading to the cucking stool is known as Ducking Stool Lane.

The rear entrance from Ye Olde George Inn, or the lane to the east of the Inn, leads to Ducking Stool Lane. The cucking stool is at the end of the lane.

Leaving Ducking Stool Lane, turning right and following Williams Street leads to the High Street. Almost directly opposite is the art deco Regent Centre for films, plays, talks, etc. The Regent Centre coffee bar is open Mondays to Saturdays 1000 – 1830. Every Friday there is a craft fair in the foyer from 1000 – 1500. Tel: 01202 499199. Next to the Regent Centre is the Tourist Information Centre. (Tel: 01202 471780).

MUSEUM OF ELECTRICTY

The museum is the only one in the UK dedicated to the history of electricity and appropriately was set up by Southern Electricity. It is located in a genuine Edwardian Power Station, believed to be the only surviving one in the UK, which was built in 1903. The exhibits are both educational and fun and guides are available to carry out demonstrations, to explain exhibits and generally add to the enjoyment.

Bournemouth used to have a tram and bus collection on display but the collection was dispersed for financial reasons in the 1990s and now most of the collection is stored in mid-Dorset although not on display to the public. The centrepiece of the collection is a fully restored 1914 tramcar which belongs to the Science Museum in London but is now on display here. A collection of photos illustrates the history of electricity generation.

The Old Power Station, Bargates, Christchurch, Dorset BH23 1QE Tel: 01202 480467. Open: Easter – to September, 1200 – 1600, Monday – Thursday. Free admission. Ample car parking.

From the Regent Centre continue north along High Street, under the flyover and into Bargates. The museum is on the right just past Beaconsfield Road.

CHRISTCHURCH PRIORY CHURCH

There was a Saxon Minster on the site around 700AD but it was demolished on the orders of William II. Prior to that there was thought to have been an important Roman building on the site. The building of an Augustinian monastery was started in 1094 and parts of this building survive to this day. It has been in continuous use as a church ever since and is said to be the largest parish church in England and is in fact larger than many of the country's cathedrals.

It escaped demolition by Henry VIII when he ordered the destruction of most of the country's monasteries. It has been described as one of the top 20 churches in the country but one which is least appreciated. The 58 ft high Nave was completed in 1150. It is the longest of any parish church and is regarded as one of the finest in England. The 15th century Bell Tower is 120 ft high and may be visited via the 176-stepped spiral staircase. St Michael's Loft

110

Museum, above the Lady Chapel, was originally a school for novice monks and later a grammar school for boys until 1869. Its exhibits depict the life of the Priory.

The town of Christchurch is said to derive its name from the events surrounding the Miraculous Beam in the Lady Chapel ambulatory. The story is told that one evening the carpenter working on the Chapel found that a beam required for the ceiling was too short. However the following morning when he arrived he

found that the beam had increased in length and had been installed. It was assumed that the mysterious carpenter who had carried out the work was Jesus Christ himself and so the church became known as Christ's Church of Twynham, as the town was then known. Subsequently the town became known simply as Christchurch. However it is believed that this story was invented by the monks in order to attract tourists who were then sold wooden objects, such as bowls, said to be made from the miraculous beam to raise funds.

Some of the oak Misericords in the Great Quire date from 1210. These small, 4½" seats were designed to give a respite from standing during the seven services the monks had to attend each 24 hours. They were purposely built to stop the monks falling asleep; if they did then the seat would fall forward with a loud noise and embarrass the offending monk. Some of the stained glass dates back to the 9th century. Below the base of the tower is a memorial to the poet Shelley which had been rejected by both Westminster Abbey and **St Peter's** in Bournemouth because it too closely resembled Christ

after being taken down from the cross.

The Priory has one of the finest organs in the South of England and a series of free lunchtime organ recitals is held during the summer on Thursdays, starting at 1230. There are periodic guided tours during the summer when visitors are shown the crypts, roof space, belfry and tower.

Open: 0930 – 1700. Loft Museum: Summer 1030 – 1230 and 1430 – 1630. Guided tours arranged with prior notice. Tel: 01202 485804.

From the Electricity Museum return along Bargate and continue on. The Priory Church is directly ahead.

RED HOUSE MUSEUM

The museum is in a Georgian building (Grade II* listed) which was used as a workhouse from 1764 until 1881 when a new house was built elsewhere in the town. It is one of only a few such workhouses to have survived to the present time. It initially housed 62 paupers but such was the demand that the number increased to 170 shortly before it closed. Part of the workhouse was used to isolate those with infectious diseases, in particular smallpox. The museum was started in 1947 and tells the story of Christchurch through the ages. The Bygone Gallery, which was the dining room,

18th century clothes dryer.

exhibits kitchen ware from the Victorian era to the 1950s. There are a variety of items charting the social and natural history of the area. The archaeological exhibits include items found on St Catherine's Hill which had been used as a lookout since pre-historic times. This includes a piece of limestone containing a painting of a fish, which was one of the earliest Christian symbols. This pre-historic display is of the highest order and is often overlooked by the casual visitor.

In the Herbert Druitt Costume Gallery is a display of wedding dresses from 1805 to 1964, as well as other items associated with weddings, although the display is shortly due to be changed to show costumes from 1901 to World War I.

One of the cabinets in the main display area is devoted to the Fusee Chain Industry that flourished in Christchurch in the 18th century. The chains, used in small time pieces, varied in length from 5" – 10" and were handmade by girls as young as nine years using the most basic of tools and without magnifying glasses. The links were so small that they could pass through the eye of a small needle. Many of the girls lived in the workhouse.

There is a walled Herb Garden and a tranquil South Garden. The roses are of historic significance and bloom for most of the year.

The Courtyard has a small café.

There is a walled Herb Garden, a tranquil South Garden and a Courtyard with a small café.

The museum runs a series of talks throughout the year, usually on a Wednesday afternoon starting at 14.00, for which there is a small charge. It is recommended that you pre-book as spaces are limited.

Red House Museum and Gardens, Quay Road, Christchurch, Dorset BH23 1BU Tel: 01202 482860. Open: Tuesday – Saturday 1000 – 1700, Sunday 1400 – 1700, closed Mondays. Free Admission.

Returning to the Priory car park, the museum is at the end of Quay Road, on the left.

STANPIT MARSH NATURE RESERVE AND TUTTON'S WELL

The Stanpit Marsh Nature Reserve consists of 150 acres of marshland and is home to over 300 species of birds and a similar number of plants. It is of national importance and said to be Christchurch's 'jewel in the crown'. It is crossed by a number of inlets and channels, the most famous of which is the 'Mother Sillers Channel', which is crossed by a Bailey bridge. (Hanna Siller, after whom the channel is named, was at one-time landlady of the Haven Inn at Mudeford Quay and was referred to as the 'Angel of the Marsh' due to the kindness she is said to have shown to smugglers.) The channel allowed smugglers to take their contraband to the Ship In Distress pub, which at the time (late 18th century) was at the edge

of the channel. The smugglers used flat-bottomed tub boats which the customs officers were unable to follow with their deeper keeled boats. The channel is reached by the footpath to the left of the Scout's hut or by walking across the field to the left. Passing through a gate leads to an information centre and the channel. The Ship in Distress pub was a favourite meeting place for smugglers and was where they stored their contraband. The two-storey part of the pub is the original building and at one stage in its history for 2½ years was used as a mortuary. Relics dating from 7000 BC have been found in the vicinity of the marsh.

A spring has existed at Tutton's Well for centuries and was the only source of fresh water on the edge of the salt water harbour. Even on the occasions when the spring or well was flooded with sea water during high tides, once the tide had receded the water in the well returned to its original purity. The water from the well is believed to be rainwater filtered down through the gravel beds in the New Forest. A tale is told that the water was sold throughout the country in the 19th century as 'The Christchurch Elixir' and was said to have excellent medicinal properties, particularly for the eyes. The water is certainly rich in iron. However the tale is thought to have been started by a local councillor around 1920. The well was given to the town in the 18th century by Sir George Rose. Approval has recently been given to renovate the well and make it more interesting for tourists to visit.

The Ship in Distress pub.

Tutton's Well.

Stanpit Marsh Nature Reserve Visitors Centre, BH23 3ND Tel: 01425 272479.

Leaving Priory car park, follow the signs to 'Town Centre'. Turn right in front of Ye Olde George Inn and travel along Castle Street, with the Castle on the right. ¾ mile further on is the Purewell Roundabout. Turn right into Stanpit and ⅓ mile on the right is the entrance and car park to Stanpit Recreation Ground, which is also an entrance to the reserve. Tutton's Well is 100 yards further along Stanpit on the right. The Ship in Distress is 50 yards in the opposite direction.

MUDEFORD

Christchurch Harbour Hotel is on the outskirts of Mudeford and is now a Grade II listed building. It was built as a gentleman's home in 1830. There are excellent views across Mudeford Quay and it is worth stopping for morning coffee, lunch or afternoon tea to enjoy the views and the recently renovated interior of the hotel.

Christchurch Harbour Hotel, Avonmouth, 95 Mudeford, Christchurch, Dorset BH23 3NT Tel: 01202 483434

From Tutton's Well, continue along Stanpit. Christchurch Harbour Hotel is ½ mile along on the right.

Mudeford has a more laid back atmosphere than its neighbours of Bournemouth and Christchurch. The village sits at the entrance to Christchurch and an enduring picture is the pile of lobster posts on the quay side. Fresh fish can be purchased from the fish stall. Ferries to Mudeford Sandbanks can be boarded from the end of the quay, as can boat tours to, or round, the Isle of Wight, to Poole and to Brownsea Island. Many people prefer the peaceful tranquillity of Mudeford to the more vibrant nature of other resorts such as Bournemouth. The area now appears to go out of its way not to promote itself – there is no Mudeford information centre, no Mudeford leaflets and it rarely, if ever, relates itself to Christchurch of which it is part.

Mudeford has a beautiful sandy beach and many other attractions. In spite of this the area has not developed in the same way as Bournemouth, Brighton and Weymouth. The name, which used to be 'Muddyford', was possibly a deterrent to visitors. Also it did not have a pier so the rich and famous of the day could not arrive by boat. It did however have a visit by George III in 1803 when, in the absence of a pier, the town's three bathing machines (see **Beach Huts**) were lined up from the shore to his boat. Also it did not help that Queen Victoria never visited the town and so it never became famous in the way that Bournemouth did. In consequence

Mudeford Quay, Christchurch BH23 4AB
Boat Tours: Adventure Voyages Tel: 01202 488662.

Continue past the hotel and ¼ mile on the right is Chichester Way, which leads to Mudeford Quay.

MUDEFORD SANDBANK

See also Bournemouth – Hengistbury Head

Mudeford Sandbank is the strip of land at the tip of Hengistbury Head which forms a natural barrier between the sea and the harbour. It is also known as Mudeford Spit (a spit is permanent land which has been formed by the deposit of sand and gravel). On one side of the strip is the Solent and the Isle of Wight and on the other Christchurch Harbour. The land is owned by Bournemouth Borough Council but was leased to Christchurch Council some years ago. The lease expires in 2029 when no doubt Bournemouth will be glad to have it back and collect the licence fees from the 350 or so beach huts. The beach huts are unique in that owners can sleep in them overnight during the summer season. Some are quite large and sleep up to six people. They have no mod cons, although there are five toilet blocks provided by the council located along the beach. Some have electricity via solar panels in their roofs. Most have either a sea view or harbour view; a few have both. They are famous for the price they can fetch when sold. In 2004 one sold for £160,000,

although prices have declined since then. At the beginning of each January 80 of the huts are rented for the coming season and people camp out for several days in order to rent one. No cars are permitted on the strip and to get there one has to walk or cycle over the windswept **Hengistbury Head**, catch the Land Train from Hengistbury Head car park, or catch the ferry from either Mudeford or Christchurch Quays. There are designated areas for swimming, paddling and watersports. The swimming and paddling areas are on the east (sea) side where the ground is sandy. The watersports area is on the west (harbour) side where the ground is rocky.

Facilities include several toilet blocks, the Beach House Café (01202 423474) and a small shop. There is also a 200 year old building called the Black House that has been converted into holiday flats.

Ferries operate from Mudeford Quay every 12 minutes during British Summer time, weather permitting, from 0900 – 1900, later at weekends. Also at weekends during winter. 1000 – 1600. Tel: 07968 334441 for details of sailing times. Dogs, cats and parrots free. See **Hengistbury Head** for details of the Land Train.

HIGHCLIFFE CASTLE

Highcliffe Castle is a magnificent Grade I Listed building. It is the second mansion to have been built on the site; the first, known as High Cliff, was built in 1773 for King George III's first Prime Minister, Lord Bute and was said to have the 'finest outlook in England'. 38 years later it had to be demolished since it had been built too close to the cliff edge. The present mansion was built between 1832 and 1835 and has been described as "The most

important remaining example of the Romantic and Picturesque style of architecture, which flourished briefly at the end of the eighteenth century and at the beginning of the nineteenth century". It was built by Lord Stuart de Rothesay, who acquired a large amount of carved medieval stonework in France and had it transported to England in twelve barges. Later he acquired quantities of medieval and eighteenth century panelling from France to decorate the rooms, as well as French furniture and carpets (some of which are now in the Victoria and Albert Museum) plus a superb collection of stained glass dating between 12th to 19th centuries, the most outstanding piece being the Jesse Window, which is a complete 16th-century window and is now in the Great Hall. The majority of the stone to

build the mansion came from the Isle of Purbeck.

After having several owners the house became a children's home, then a seminary until it was sold in 1967. Two fires severely damaged the castle and it remained empty for 10 years until purchased in 1978 by Christchurch Borough Council to safeguard its existence. Severe storms in 1990 further damaged the building. Repair work finally started with the help of English Heritage in 1994 and its doors were opened to the public for the first time in 1995.

The castle holds a series of lectures, exhibitions and events; check beforehand if you want to attend. There is a coastal path that runs from Mudeford Quay to Chewton Bunny. The 2.5 mile walk along the cliff-top passes through the Steamer Point Nature Reserve and the grounds of Highcliffe Castle. The cliffs are a site of Special Scientific Interest.

Highcliffe Castle, Rothesay Drive, Highcliffe, Dorset BH23 4LE. Tel: 01425 278807. Open: Feb & March: 1100 – 1600 weekends only; April – October 1100 – 1700 daily; Nov – 23 Dec 1100 – 1600 daily. Admission to the grounds is free and permits visitors to wander through the gardens and walk down the zigzag to the sea.

Leaving Mudeford from Chichester Way, turn right and after 100 yards turn left into Bure Lane. Continue for one mile. Turn right at the roundabout onto the A337 and the road leading to Highcliffe Castle is ¾ mile on the right.
Wilts & Dorset Bus numbers 121, 122 or 123 Bournemouth go direct to the castle.

SAMMY MILLER MOTORCYCLE MUSEUM

The earliest machine is the 1898 Quadrant shown above.

Sammy Miller has been the most successful motorcycle trials rider during the last 50 years, having been British Champion eleven times and European Champion twice. He started racing competitively in 1951 at the age of 16. He was awarded the MBE in 2009 for services to motorcycle heritage. The museum was started in 1964 after Sammy set up a spare parts business and it has continued to grow. It is now probably the finest such museum in the world housing more than 300 restored rare and classic motorcycles. The machines are ridden in live bike events throughout the world. Sammy continues to search for new exhibits from all over the world and they tend to arrive monthly so the display continues to grow. In almost all cases the exhibits have to be renovated before being displayed. Even in his seventies, Sammy is still actively involved in restoring the machines and in riding them. The museum is well worth a visit.

Sammy Miller Motorcycle Museum, Bashley Cross Road, New Milton, Hampshire, BH25 5SZ. Tel: 01425 620777 Open: All week 1000 – 1630. Weekends only in winter. Small café, children's play area and animal farm including some alpacas and donkeys.

On leaving Hichcliffe Castle turn right onto the A337. 200 yards further on turn left into Castle Avenue. 1 mile further turn right onto A35. ¾ mile further turn right into the B3055. The museum is 1¼ miles on the right. From Bournemouth, take the A35. 4 miles past the double Fountain Roundabout turn right onto B3055. The museum is 1¼ miles on the right. See also the New Forest Trail (page 128).

BEACH HUTS

Beach huts are a British invention, dating from around the beginning of the 20th century. The first purpose-built ones are believed to have been erected in Bournemouth in 1908 on either side of the pier and were designed by the Bournemouth Borough's Engineer at the time. A few of the present huts still retain some of the original features. Hut 2357, to the east of Bournemouth Pier, is believed to be the oldest, although not much of the originl hut remains.

The use of the seaside for recreational purposes is a relatively modern phenomenon. Prior to that the beach was only used by fishermen and smugglers. This changed when in the 18th century doctors began to recommend a spell in the cold sea as a remedy for almost any ailment and the whole family accompanied the patient to the seaside. Men and women had to use separate beaches and the patient was expected to go naked into the sea. To get over any embarrassment this nakedness might cause, the 'bathing machine' was invented. This was a carriage on wheels. The patient would undress in the carriage at the top of the beach, which would be pulled into the sea by a horse. The front of the carriage would be lowered and the patient 'helped' into the sea by attendants. In 1789 George III had the use of one in Weymouth, as an attempt was made to cure his madness by immersing him in the cold sea. Frequent use of the bathing machine by the king gave them an air of respectability. In fact at this time bathing costumes had not been thought of and everyone went naked into the sea, usually by hiring a bathing machine. At this time, people did not swim but simply were immersed, or immersed themselves, in the sea for a short period of time.

By the turn of the 20th century it had become acceptable for men and women to use the same beach although it was not very acceptable for them to change into swimming cloths on the beach. The machines were therefore used by the wealthy to give them privacy, although it was necessary to keep an appropriate distance between the male and female bathing machines. Queen Victoria had her own personal bathing machine built on the Isle of Wight. It was a relatively natural progression to having first temporary beach tents on the sea shore as shown in the 1900 picture below, and then permanent beach huts which served the same purpose and local councils were able to raise revenue by having them built and renting them out.

Today there are believed to be around 20,000 beach huts in the UK, most owned or leased by the relevant local authority. They have changed little over the years. Most are wooden built, brightly painted and have the barest of facilities.

EAST HURN

The small village of Hurn is five miles north-east of Bournemouth, lying between the Rivers Stour and Avon. It is mentioned in the Domesday Book as 'Herne' and derives its name from the old English word 'hyrne' meaning a 'disused part of a field'. It lies within the Borough of Christchurch although is some distance from Christchurch itself.

If you have considered learning to fly then the **BOURNEMOUTH FLYING CLUB** based in East Hurn offers trial lessons

lasting between 30 and 60 minutes. The club was formed in the 1930s and now has 10 aircraft. They do not have a sightseeing licence but if you take a trial lesson you can always opt not to take the controls. They try to accommodate the route you would like to fly but there are restrictions due to the proximity of the airport and the army's firing range along part of the Purbeck Coast. The Flying Club has a small café and restaurant directly overlooking the runway.

Bournemouth Flying Club, Aviation Park East, Matchams Lane, Bournemouth Airport, Christchurch, Dorset BH23 6NE. Tel: 01202 578558.

Take the A338 Ringwood Road. A half mile beyond the speed limit derestriction sign turn left on the B3073, signposted Bournemouth Airport. 200 yards further on turn right and continue for another half mile to the roundabout. Turn right (second exit) and 100 yards further on take the second exit (Matchams Lane). The turning to the Aviation Park East is ½ mile along on the left. Bournemouth Flying Club is ½ mile along on the left.

A further attraction near East Hurn are the ski slopes at **SNOWTRAX**. The combined slopes are the widest in the country and are set in grounds with a lake and pine trees. The slopes have artificial bumps and a unique mist-lubricating system. There is a choice of skiing, snowboarding, ski-bobbing (minimum age 5) or ringoing (minimum age 3, minimum height 3 feet). Lessons are available for each activity for those who require them, including advanced skiing lessons. There is also a good licensed restaurant

At the bottom of the Ski Slopes is an Alpine Adventure Park set among trees and suitable for youngsters of all ages. Activities include trampolines, alpine fort, swings, cable ride, mini assault course and toddlers' play area.

Snowtrax, Matchams Lane, Hurn, Christchurch, Dorset BH23 6AW. Tel: 01202 499155. Open daily from 1000 – 2200 daily all year but there is restricted use at certain times so contact the centre before going.

Snowtrax is ¾ mile past the turning to Bournemouth Aviation Park East, on the right.

MATCHAMS LEISURE PARK is also at Hurn and the main activity here is Karting, which takes place every day other than Mondays. Here young (minimum age 14) and old can drive the 200cc, four stroke, Biz Karts and train to become the next Lewis Hamilton. The karts can reach a maximum speed of 50mph on the 420 metre track. You can normally just arrive and drive, although you are advised to phone beforehand to check availability. Prices depend on the time spent on the track. On a cold or wet day an indoors area allows non-riders to watch the events in comfort. Light refreshments are available.

Close by is a 100 metre track for fun karts, which can travel at up to 25 mph. The minimum age for riding these is 8, with a minimum height requirement of 1.3 metres.

The Kart Circuit, Matchams Leisure Park, Matchams Lane, Hurn, Nr Ringwood BH24 2BT. Tel: 07851 730000.

Mathams Park is 1 mile past Snowtrax on the left. The Kart Circuit is at the end of the road.

Occasionally there are other activities at the park. For details contact Matchams Leisure Park, Hurn Road, Nr Ringwood, Dorset BH24 2BT. Tel: 01273 564264.

WEST HURN

BOURNEMOUTH AIRPORT, also known as Hurn Airport, is located in West Hurn and is actually in the Borough of Christchurch. However, like Bournemouth University which is in Poole, the airport borrows the name of its larger and better known neighbour. Bournemouth Council had been recommended to build an airport at Hurn in 1931 but did nothing. However when the government were looking for new airfields in 1939 Hurn was recommended and work on building the airport began the same year. RAF Hurn opened with three runways in 1941 and played a vital role during the Second World War. Initially it was used solely for gliders but towards the end of the war it became a base for Mosquitos and Typhoons. In 1944 BOAC started tests for converting the Lancaster bomber to a passenger carrying civilian aircraft and the first passenger flight (to Egypt) from Hurn Airport took place the same year, as did one to Australia with a journey time of more than two

significantly. Since then the airport, now known as Bournemouth International Airport, has extended its runway and has one of the longest runways in the country.

The airport has expanded significantly in the last few years with the advent of budget airlines and at the present time the main carrier is Ryanair. The airport is currently undergoing a multi-million pound refurbishment, which is due for completion in 2010 and the passenger numbers are expected to increase from the present one million a year to three million by 2015. In a recent poll the airport was voted the third best airport in the world! One airline has its home at the airport, namely Palmair, which has just one plane and in 2008 won the 'Best Short Carrier' award.

Bournemouth Airport, Christchurch, Dorset. BH23 6NW.

Take the A338 Wessex Way, Ringwood Road. ½ mile beyond the speed limit derestricion sign turn left on the B3073, signposted Bournemouth Airport. After 100 yards turn right and continue for another ½ mile to the roundabout. Turn left (first exit) and the airport is ½ mile further on the right.

days. By the following year Hurn was the largest civilian long-haul airport in the UK with all major passenger airlines using it. But in 1946 Heathrow opened and passenger flights from Hurn declined

Also at West Hurn is **ADVENTURE WONDERLAND** which combines the Alice in Wonderland Theme Park and the Aztec Play Centre. The park claims to be Dorset's Number 1 Theme Park and has won Bournecoast Top Children's Attraction award for two years in succession. There is an excellent Alice in Wonderland Maze, with one and a half miles of paths and seven foot high beech hedging to prevent cheating and claims to be the largest maze on the south coast. Those who have difficulty in solving it can answer the series of questions within it to find a quicker route out. The park has a large number of games based on the Alice in Wonderland story with some exciting outdoor rides. The Happydrome Theatre has shows at 1200 and 1500 when there is a variety of entertainers. The attraction

This Hawker Hunter took part in the 1958 Farnborough air show when together with another 21 of them they looped the loop, still a record in the Guinness Book of Records.

includes an indoor Aztec Play Centre known as 'Wild Thing' which cost over £1 million to build with over 20 different rides and attractions.

The Mad Hatter's Café, in the Alice building, is open every day from 1030 – 1700 with hot meals from 1130 – 1500. The café in Wild Thing is open from 1000 – 1700 serving drinks, fast foods, salads and snacks.

Adventure Wonderland, Merritown Lane, Hurn, Dorset BH23 6BA Tel: 01202 483444. Open: Adventure Wonderland from March – September 1000 – 1800 (last entry 1600). Wild Thing: All year 1000 – 1830 (last entry 1700).

Follow the directions to Bournemouth Airport and the attraction is a further ½ mile on the left.

Sharing the ground with Adventure Wonderland is the **AVIATION MUSEUM** which opened in 1998 in the grounds of Bournemouth Airport where, for nine years, it was a successful attraction showing vintage and classic aircraft. Unfortunately the museum was forced to close in December 2007 when the Airport required the land for a car park as part of its expansion. Fortunately the museum was offered space in the grounds of Adventure Wonderland, although the space only permits a limited number of exhibits of vintage static aircraft and cockpits. The museum is now looking for a larger and more suitable site where once again flying aircraft and engineering activities can be accommodated.

On display are a number of classic planes, including piston powered trainers and a Naval Rescue helicopter. The cockpits include those of the Lightning Fighter and the Vulcan Bomber. A sit-in flight simulator allows hands-on experience of flying. A small shop sells books, models and other aviation items. The museum plans to create an Aviation Heritage Centre with both flying and

Chichester-Miles Leopard, one of only two in existence.

123

static planes. In addition there are plans to have details of aviation history and technology with the emphasis on educating young people. The museum is run entirely by volunteers. If you want a guide then one will be provided free of charge. There is also a double-decker bus that gives a good view of the airport from the upper deck.

The museum is in the same grounds as the Adventure Wonderland.

Beyond the Adventure Wonderland is Aviation Park West which accommodates the **SOLENT SCHOOL OF FLYING** where trial flying lessons are offered. (Tel: 01202 582181). **BOURNE-MOUTH HELICOPTERS** offer trial lessons with a minimum flight time of 20 minutes. (Tel 01202 590800). Participants do not necessary have to take contraol of the helicopter and, within reason, can fly wherever they wish. The firm are soon hoping to offer sight-seeing flights when they have the necessary licence. To obtain a full licence requires 45 hours of flying. This will cost about £7,500 for a small aircraft and about twice that for a helicopter.

Aviation Park West, Bournemouth Airport, Christchurch, Dorset, BH23 6NW.

For the Aviation Park West, go 1½ miles past the entrance to Bournemouth Airport and then turn right at the roundabout. Bournemouth Helicopters and the Solent Flying School are 1½ miles along the road after passing through the barrior.

DOBWALL STEAM TRAINS, based at Plowman's Nursery & Plant Centre, is located just outside Hurn. Here there is an excellent collection of eight locomotives (four steam and four diesel) which are replicas of American trains, built from plans of the original locomotives and built to a ratio of 8 to 1. It is the largest collection of such trains in the world and the cost of making the models today

would be several million pounds. They run on over 2,000 yards of track. The owner of the nursery purchased them in 2008 from their previous owner who exhibited them in Cornwall. During their 35 years in Cornwall they carried more than 7 million passengers.

Plowman's Nursery & Plant Centre, West Parley, Ferdown, BH22 8SW. Tel 01202 582169.

Continue along the B3073 past Adventure Wonderland. After 1½ miles turn left at the roundabout and the nursery is ½ mile on the left.

RINGWOOD

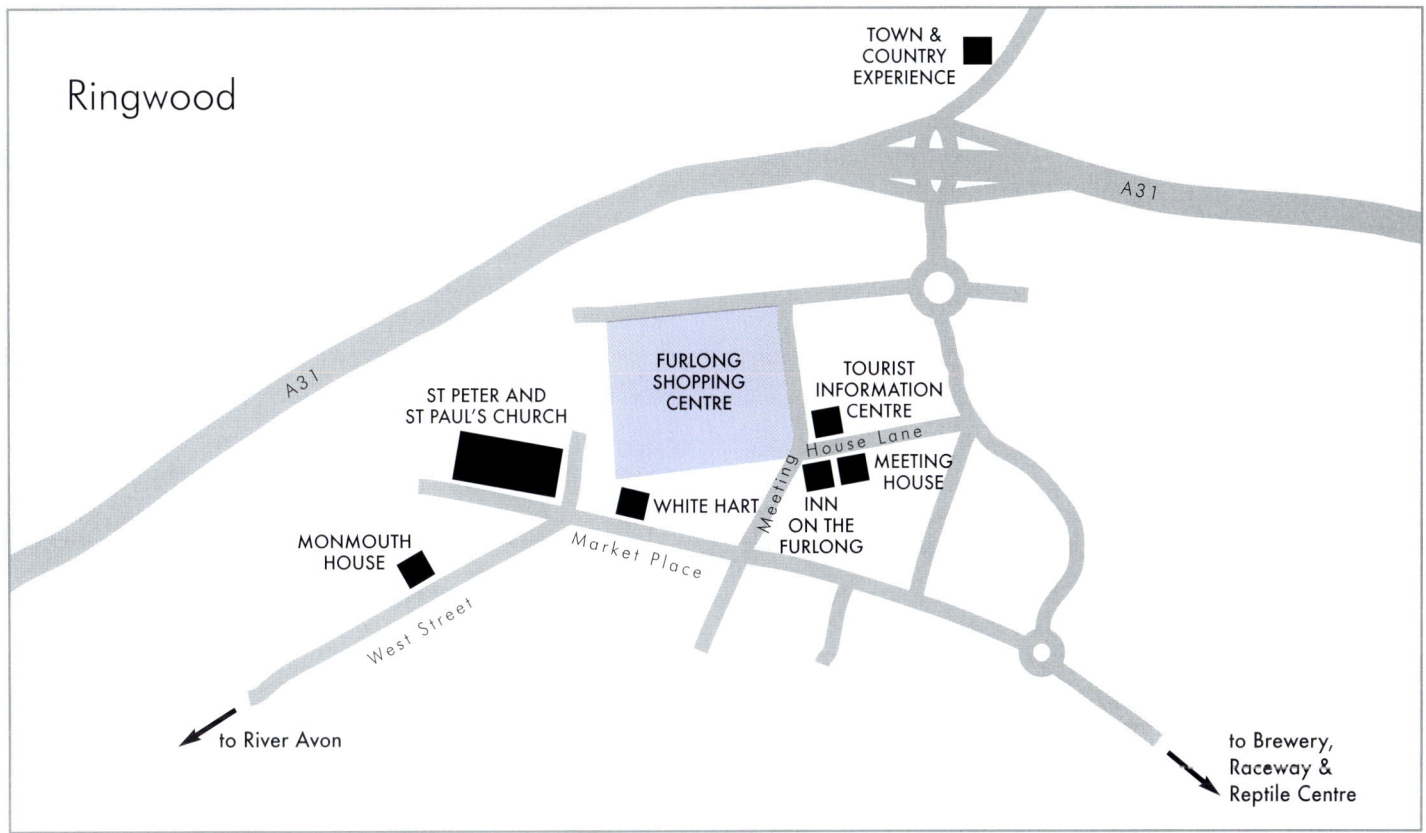

Ringwood is located at the western entrance to the New Forest. The town dates back to around the year 1000 and there is a brief mention of it in the Domesday Book of 1086 when it was known as Rincewed.

In 1226 King Henry III granted the manor the right to hold a market each week on a Wednesday and for several hundred years it was the main market in the area, especially with regard to the selling of Forest ponies. Although the market continues to this day, the sale of livestock has long since ceased. The site which was the livestock market is now the Furlong Shopping Precinct and its bronze sculpture of a mare and foal is a reminder of the town's history.

Close by, and opposite the Tourist Information Centre, is the Ringwood Meeting House which was built in 1727 for the local Presbyterian dissenters. It remains virtually the same as it was at the time it was built and is considered to be one of the best meeting houses remaining in the country. It has Grade II* listing. Many of the pews are fixed in squares so that some worshipers would sit with their backs to the minister. When it was built the site was far removed from the centre of Ringwood, unlike today where it is in the heart of the town. During the 19th century the congregation became Unitarian and the place of worship became known as St Thomas' Chapel. It reverted back to its original name in 1933 and

and several breweries were set up. Ringwood was a major staging post for coaches travelling to London from the south coast and at this time there were said to be more pubs in Ringwood than any other town in the country. Men and women drank more ale at this time than water since the ale was safer to drink due to the sterilization process it underwent, whereas water would frequently be

contaminated. The tradition of brewing continues to this day with **Ringwood Brewery**. The Inn on the Furlong pub, next to the Meeting House, is owned by the Ringwood Brewery; it used to be the home of the minister of the Meeting House.

Walking down Meeting House lane, leads to Market Place where the Wednesday market is now held. A short way along is the White Hart Hotel (Tel: 01425 472702) which claims to be the 'original' White Hart. It is said that a white hart was chased by King Henry VII's hunting party but when the ladies in the party saw the magnificence of the beast they begged for it to be spared. This was done and when the party went to the local hostelry for a drink and the owner heard about the deer he changed the name of his establishment.

Further along Market Place is the Grade II* listed Ringwood Parish Church of St Peter and St Paul, which is a well known

closed for religious use in 1975. It opened again for public use in 1986. Its clock, dated 1730, was stolen in 2002.

Open from Monday to Friday between 1000 and 1200. There is a 50p entry fee which includes a cup of tea or coffee. It is being developed as an interesting small museum and exhibition centre, mainly in the upper gallery. Tel: 01425 472315.

Towards the beginning of the 18th century it was realised that water from the River Avon was ideal for use in the brewing of beer

landmark that can be seen when driving to Bournemouth from the East. It dates from 1855 and has a beautiful interior. Outside is the Jubilee Lamp, erected in 1887 to commemorate Queen Victoria's Golden Jubilee. It originally had gas lamps, a water trough for use by animals and four fountains with chained water cups; there are plans to restore it to its original form.

On the death of Charles II in 1685, his younger brother James II claimed the throne. The protestant and well liked Duke of Monmouth was the illegitimate son of Charles II and he believed that he should be king, rather than the Roman Catholic and unpopular James II. He had himself crowned king at Chard, the ancient capital of Wessex. On 6th July 1685 James II challenged and defeated the Duke of Monmouth at the Battle of Sedgemoor, a battle that is usually regarded as England's last civil war. After his defeat at Sedgemoor, Monmouth was captured and held in what is now known as Monmouth House (located towards the end of West Street), before being taken to the Tower of London, tried for treason and executed on 15th July 1685 when it took between five and eight blows from the axe to remove his head. Papers in the Ringwood Meeting House's museum state that after the duke's beheading it was

realised that there was no portrait of him. This was clearly unacceptable since he was the son of a king, even if an illegitimate one. His head was therefore sewn back on and a portrait of him painted, which is now in the National Portrait Gallery in London. Another exhibit in the museum states that this story is untrue.

Next to Monmouth House is an 11th century thatched cottage now housing the Old Cottage Restaurant (Tel: 01425 474283) and beyond this is Jubilee Gardens.

The stone, three-arched bridge over the River Avon once carried the main road between London and the South-West of England and in particular to and from the thriving town of Poole.

Take the A338 Ringwood Road from Bournemouth. At the roundabout, six miles beyond the speed derestriction sign on the outskirts of Bournemouth, turn right (third exit) onto the A31. One mile further on take the left fork (B3347) signposted to Ringwood. Turn right at the roundabout (third exit). Keep on the B3347 across the next roundabout and into Ringwood.

NEW FOREST TRAIL

Often a 'forest' conjures up pictures of an area of dense trees and although the New Forest, which was created by King William in 1079, does have dense areas of trees, a large part of it is impoverished and will only support heathland, wetland and grazing land; these areas are referred to as the Open Forest. The notion of a forest dates back to the time of William the Conqueror and refers to an area of land where the king had rights to all the natural resources in the area, including livestock. Most of the Forest is still owned by the Crown and is managed by the Forestry Commission, with part being owned by the National Trust and a small part by individuals. Many people have grazing rights for their livestock (although only female animals are allowed to roam freely) and they are known as 'commoners'. These grazing rights arose since the king did not permit areas to be fenced as this would have interfered with his hunting of the deer and boar. The following is a trail which will introduce you to parts of the New Forest.

Sopley Mill.

Take the Wessex Way (A338) Ringwood Road from Bournemouth. ½ mile beyond the speed limit deristriction sign, turn left on the B3073, signposted Bournemouth Airport. After a further 200 yards turn right and continue for another ½ mile to the roundabout. Turn right (second exit) towards Sopley. Continue for just over 1½ miles and then turn right onto the B3347. Continue for ¾ mile and then turn right toward the Wool Pack. Immediately turn left in front of the Wool Pack and Sopley Mill is ¼ mile further on – the road becomes gravel after a short distance.

St Michael and All Angels.

Sopley Mill dates from 1878 although there is thought to have been a mill on the site since the time of the Domesday Book in 1086. Milling ceased around 1955. The mill is now a restaurant and well worth a visit. The stream that used to drive the mill separates from the River Avon upstream, before rejoining it down stream and was famous for its eels.

On the lane that leads to the Mill is the entrance to **St Michael and All Angels Church**, parts of which date from the 12th century,

although almost certainly a small church was on the site in the 11th century. The present church is built of ironstone rubble, probably taken from Hengistbury Head. Just before entering the church, to the left of the porch on the eaves of the south wing, can be seen a Sheela-na-Gig. There are only 45 of these in the UK – there is another at Studland church – and they date from the 12th century. They normally depict women showing an extremely exaggerated vulva, as in the one on the west eave of the porch. Male Sheela-na-

Gigs are very rare and the one here can be clearly seen holding his legs apart to show his genitals. There are several theories as to thir significance – they are warning against lusts of the flesh, they are warding off evil spirits, they are the Celtic pagan goddess Cailleach, they are fertility figures shown to women on their wedding day.

Beside the main road is the **Woolpack Inn** parts of which date from 1725 although the thatched part is from several years later. The building was used by the military during the Second World War and General Eisenhower and Winston Churchill are said to have had meetings here before going underground in a nearby bunker.

The Woolpack Inn.

From Sopley Mill return to the Wool Pack and follow the one way system. After 300 yards turn right and rejoin the B3347. After 200 yards turn left towards Bransgore. After 1¼ miles you come to the entrance to Merryfield Park.

Merryfield Park was part of Winkton Airfield which opened in 1943 in preparation for the D-day landing. The airfield, known as **Winkton Advanced Landing Ground**, was used by 9th Air Force of the United States Army and housed 1000 airmen with 75 aircraft

Merryfield Park.

belonging to three squadrons. From 1952–74 the camp was used by the RAF including use by the Household Cavalry for Rest and Recuperation and then in 1977 as a reception centre for the Vietnamese Boat People. Many of the huts used by the military are still here, including the Guard House and NAAFI Although the area is in private hands, visitors are usually able to explore the site; many of the huts have fallen into a state of disrepair. The site has recently been sold, subject to the necessary planning permission, although it could take several years before any development takes place.

The park is home of the **New Forest Airfields Education and Interpretation Centre** which is in the same building as the Reception. The centre is dedicated to the study of the various New Forest airfields. During World War II there were 12 airfields built in the New Forest and used by the Americans, British and Canadians. Only the one at Hurn remains and is now known as Bournemouth International Airport. The centre has a collection of books, photographs, prints etc and talks are given to local schools by its members.

New Forest Airfields Education and Interpretation Centre, Merryfield Park, Derritt Lane, Bransgore BH23 8AU. Tel: 01425 674516. Admission free. Viewing by appointment.

On leaving Merryfield Park turn left. After ½ mile turn right at the T-junction. After a further ⅓ mile continue over the crossroads into Ringwood Road. ¼ mile further on the left is St Mary the Virgin Church, in the village of Bransgore.

St Mary the Virgin Church was built in 1822 with the chancel dating from 1873. The churchyard has a number of interesting headstones, with a poignant row of them to babies and small children. One of the past vicars was Henry Willberforce whose father, William, was to the fore in the fight to abolish slavery. The church is one of over 600 churches that was built out of £1 million given by the government in 1818 as a thanks for the victory at the Battle of Waterloo which ended the Napoleonic Wars. Building costs were to be kept to the minimum. The churches are known as 'Waterloo Churches'.

St Mary the Virgin.

Revd. Rickman, St. Mary's Vicarage, Ringwood Rd, Bramsgrove. Tel: 01425 672327

Return to the crossroads and turn right along Burley Road. The Church of All Saints is 1¼ mile along on the left.

The Grade I listed All Saints, Thorney Hill was built by Lord Manners of Avon Tyrrell in 1906. The church has a north-south orientation. The roof was covered in lead but the lead was stolen in 1966 and replaced with aluminium. However the aluminium had many pin-holes and so was not watertight and with the help of

All Saints' Church.

National Heritage, in 2005 the aluminium was replaced once more with lead. The bell tower was designed so that smoke from the candles that illuminated the inside of the church was vented through it.

Four giant Tuscan columns support the roof. In the semi-circular apse is a mural painted in 1922 by Phoebe Traquair and was her last great work. So the mural could cover the entire apse, the windows on the south wall were blocked in. All 38 figures depicted in the mural are images of real people, including the children looking down from the dome who were from the local school. There is a problem with dampness and in the restoration process part of the painting has been sacrificed so that the wall can dry out at that point. The lack of trees in the church grounds is the result of a violent storm in 1991 when around 145 of them, some over 100 years old, were

The apse in All Saints.

continued, although the gypsies have since been housed in council accommodation.

To view the church Tel: 01425 672247.

On leaving All Saints' Church continue along Burley Road for ¼ mile and then turn left signposted Avon Tyrell. The drive leading to Avon Tyrell is ⅓ mile further on the right and the house ½ mile down the drive.

Avon Tyrell was built for Lord Manners in 1891 and is considered one of the finest houses of that time. It is Grade I listed. The home was donated by Lord Manners in 1949 to the 'Youth of the Nation' and it is now the head office of UK Youth. The grounds extend to 65 acres and include an artificial lake. The house was built on the money Lord Manners made from a bet, which was that he could buy, train and ride the winner of the 1882 Grand National, which was a matter of months away. Few believed he could do it and the horse started at odds of 10-1. At the final fence his horse, Seaman, went lame and had to be nursed past the finishing post but nevertheless won, from the favourite, by a short head. The prize money of £28,000 paid for both the building of the house and of All Saints' Church. The horse is said to be buried in the grounds. The house is referred to as the 'calendar' house because it has 365 windows, 52 rooms, 12 chimneys and 7 outside doors. The main entrance hall has a marble fireplace containing fossils while the ceilings in this and some of the other rooms are outstanding for their ornate plasterwork.

blown down. The war memorial was also damaged but has since been repaired.

The graveyard is interesting in that many of the graves have displays of flowers which, on inspection, are seen to be artificial. Many of the early worshipers were gypsies who were hired to look after the brick-makers' kilns at night and they were buried in the church's graveyard. Flowers have always played a large part in their lives and the tradition of having artificial flowers on the graves has

Avon Tyrell House.

Avon Tyrell Activity Centre, UK Youth, Bransgore, Hampshire BH23 8EE. Tel: 01425 672347. Short guided tours of house and grounds arranged by appointment.

Return to Burley Road and go straight across into Forest Road. After ½ mile turn right into Black Lane. The New Forest Airfields Memorial is ⅔ mile on the right.

Holmsley South Airfield opened in 1942. Initially it was home for the Halifax Bomber but towards the end of the war was home to Spitfires and Typhoons. The airfield closed in 1946 but is now the site of the **Airfields Memorial**, which stands as a tribute to the work carried out at these airfields. The memorial, which is faced with Portland Stone, was dedicated in 2002. A map on the site gives the location of all 12 airfields. (The post code that takes you nearest to the Memorial is BH23 8EB.)

New Forest Airfields, Memorial.

After leaving the memorial continue to the road junction and turn right. After ⅓ mile turn left at the T-junction and after ½ mile turn right (south) onto the A35. The church of St Michael and All Angels is 1½ miles along the road. The road to the left just before the church leads after 1⅓ mile to Sammy Miller's Motorcycle Museum (see page 118).

St Michael and All Angels' Church, Hinton, which is approached through a lych gate and a lime-tree lined path, contains a beautiful 13 arched, Portland stone reredos. The organ dates from 1875 and the decoration on its 28 pipes still looks fresh. A private path links the church with Hinton Admiral, the home of the Meyrick family who played a major part in the development of Bournemouth.

The nave of the church was built in 1774 as a chapel and paid for by Joseph Jarvis Clerke who owned much of the land in the area. On his death in 1778 the estate passed to his great nephew George Ivison Tapps. (George's parents had officially married 18 years after his birth when his father was a frail 69 year old. It is interesting that George's initials spell the old English word 'git' meaning 'bastard'.) George Tapps was granted a Baronetcy, in 1791 and in 1810 he sold 8½ acres of land on the west bank of the Bourne Stream to Lewis Tregonwell, the founder of Bournemouth. The second baronet added the surname Gervis to Tapps and in the 1870s refurbished and enlarged the chapel to the church seen today. He also developed the east bank of Bournemouth's Bourne Stream. The third Baronet

St Michael and All Angels, Hinton.

added the name Meyrick to his title following a bequest of many acres of land from a relative, Owen Meyrick. It was this third Baronet, known as Sir George Eliott Meyrick Tapps-Gervis-Meyrick, who played a major part in the development of Bournemouth. He was instrumental in establishing Bournemouth's first local government authority, the building of Bournemouth's pier and, most importantly for the development of the town, in permitting the new railway line from Bournemouth to London to pass through his land. Meyrick Park, which was the first of Bournemouth's public parks, is named after him. The Meyrick estate still owns land in Bournemouth, including parts of the Bournemouth's Lower Gardens and sea front.

To view Tel: 01425 615620.

On leaving the church return north along the A35 for 3 miles and then turn left. The Station House Restaurant is on the right.

The Station House Restaurant.

The Station House restaurant was the Holmsley Railway Station and is one of the many places in the area where you can buy a cream tea. Appropriately the various teas are called the Gate Keeper's, Signalman's, Porter's, Ticket Inspector's, Station Master's and Station House, all priced differently.

Continue and after a further 100 yards turn left and the road leads after 2 miles, direct to Burley.

Moorhill House Hotel.

On the outskirts of Burley, and before entering the village itself, is the entrance to the Moorhill House Hotel (Tel: 01425 403285) the dedicated road to the hotel takes you deep into the Forest. Although the building is not too impressive from the outside, the interior is attractive, and their excellent Sunday lunches and cream teas are less expensive than some of those on offer in the centre of the village.

The name 'Burley' is from the Saxon word meaning 'the fortified village in the clearing' and refers to an Iron Age camp which was close to the present village. It is one of the most picturesque villages in the New Forest and there will almost certainly be ponies walking in the roads and holding up the traffic. Burley has a strong connection with witches and there are several shops selling items associated with witchcraft. The village's most famous witch of modern times was

Sybil Leek who in the 1950s would walk in the village in her long, black robe with a jackdaw on her shoulder. She later moved to America.

The road to the left in front of the war memorial and cross, leads after 200 yards to the Village Hall on the right and after a further 100 yards to New Forest Cider on the left. There are three examples of early cider presses on display, including the Workman Steam Driven Press dating from 1890. All are used on one weekend every October, although most of the pressing is carried out on a modern press. Visitors are able to sample the various types of cider.

The road to the right passing the war memorial and cross on the left, leads after 200 yards to the entrance of the Burley Manor Hotel. (Tel: 01425 403522). One of the early Burleys was executed in the Tower of London and the estates passed to the king. The present building dates from 1852 and it became a hotel in 1932. If you are fortunate you may see a herd of red deer grazing in the meadow in front of the hotel.

Burley Manor Hotel.

134

The oldest building in the village is the 17th century Queen's Head, which faces you at the entrance to the village. It was a favourite haunt for smugglers in the 18th and 19th centuries. Deer Park Safaris and horse-drawn wagon rides leave from the car park next to the pub during the summer season.

Leave the village on Chapel Lane which passes in front of the Queen's Head and a few hundred yards on the right is Church Lane leading to St John the Baptist Church, set in the midst of the forest.

St John the Baptist Church.

St John the Baptist Church dates from 1839 and, lying as it does amongst dense trees, is worth a visit, as well as to see its beautiful interior and stained glass windows. The Millennium Window, directly opposite the entrance, was paid for by a collection from the whole village.

Continue on Church Road for 5 miles and turn left on the A35. After ¼ mile turn right into Rhinefield Ornamental Drive.

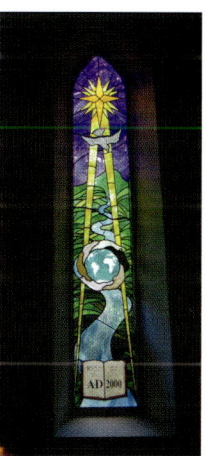

The drive along the Rhinefield Ornamental Drive takes you through a most beautiful part of the New Forest and after 1½ miles to the Rhinefield House Hotel. The house was built in the late 1880s and stayed in the same family until death duties forced its sale in 1950. After a succession of owners and uses the house was turned into a hotel in 1982 and today is a mixture of hotel and time-share apartments. It is an outstanding building and the Grand Hall reminds visitors of Westminster Hall. The Alhambra Room in particular is spectacular and is an exact copy of the Alhambra Palace in Granada. It had been built by the owner as a wedding present for her husband who had so admired the Alhambra Palace on their honeymoon. It should not be missed. The trees in the grounds include beautiful giant redwoods.

Rhinefield House Hotel.

The road continues past the hotel for another mile before coming once more to open forest. However on leaving the hotel return along the Rhinefield Ornamental Drive to the A35 and continue straight across to the Bolderwood Arboretum Ornamental Drive, said to be the road with the longest name in England. The Drive passes through another magnificent part of the Forest. After 2½ miles the Bolderwood car park is on the right. A path on the opposite side of the road leads to a deer sanctuary.

Chritax Taxis do fixed price Cream Tea tours that cover much of the New Forest Trail. Tel: 08000 858607.

To return to Bournemouth, turn right on leaving the car park and then after 200 yards left and continue for about 8 miles when you can join the A31.

MOORS VALLEY COUNTRY PARK

To the northwest of Ringwood is the very popular Moors Valley Country Park. East Dorset District Council purchased an 82 acre farm in 1984 and installed a narrow-gauge railway, a visitors centre, a 9-hole golf course, a lake and a play area. The park opened to the public for the first time four years later and was so successful that the Council purchased a further 170 acres, increased the golf course to 18 holes, constructed a second lake and created a tree top

trail. The park now receives more than 750,000 visitors per year. The Visitors Centre is in an 18th century timber barn and also houses the Seasons Restaurant, a shop, the cycle hire centre, an information point and the warden's office. A map giving the layout of the park is available from the centre.

Both the Visitors Centre (Tel: 01425 470721) and restaurant (Tel: 01425 470537) are open from 0900 to 1630.

The 18-hole, par 72, pay-and-play golf course runs along the Moors River valley. In addition there is a four-hole pitch and putt course, practice nets and a chipping green. Boules, croquet and putting are also available.

Moors Valley Golf Club. Tel: 01425 479776. Hours are from 0800 to dusk. Charges vary depending on the time of day. To reach the golf club turn left soon after entering the park and proceed through the barrier.

There is an adventure play area for older children, another play area suitable for the very young, as well as clearly labelled walks and cycle routes. Cycles can be hired from the Information Centre from 0930 – 1530. The permanent all year round orienteering courses

are designed for those on foot, on mountain bikes or in wheelchairs. Prior details can be obtained from the park ranger at the visitors centre.

The forest has a mile long Play Trail. It allows you to explore inside a giant 'ants nest', crawl through 'towers and tunnels', slide inside the 'snake pit', try the 'crocodile crossing' and wind your way through the 'pond maze'. A tree top trial 5 metres high is accessible from this play trail.

The **Go Ape** aerial assault course is set high amongst the trees. Full instructions are given at the start of the course and you are fitted with a safety harness at all times. Instructors do not

The **Moors Valley Railway** opened to the public in 1986 having taken a year to construct. Most of the locomotives, rolling stock and workshop machinery were transferred from a site in Christchurch which had closed. Some of the original farm buildings on the site were converted for use by the railway, so for example the cow shed became Kingsmere Station. This building includes a café and a small shop selling items for model railways. Kingsmere is the main station, while the station close to the information centre is Lakeside. The trains run on 7¼ inch gauge, aluminium track. There is about one and a half mile of track, although the section over which the passenger trains travels is about a mile. The journey goes along the banks of the Moors Lake, through three tunnels, up a steep gradient (one wonders whether the train is going to make it), round fairly sharp bends and over a bridge. You can alight at either station or travel directly back. In off-peak times the ticket office at Lakeside Station may not be staffed and on these occasions the trains do not stop and only round trips are possible. The total journey time for the round trip is about 20 minutes. The signal men and drivers are volunteers, whereas the shop workers and guard are paid. The usual guard is 85 year old Kenneth Clay who has been collecting tickets, signalling the train off and advising passengers where to alight for 17 years.

accompany you on the course, although they are available should you get stuck. Participants leave in small groups at 30 minute intervals. There is no time limit but the course normally takes about three hours. It is in sections and you are able to leave at the end of each section and return to base. The highest point is 36 ft and the longest slide wire 545 ft. The site has more than 30,000 visitors a year and, judging by the howls of pleasure, is great fun. The oldest person to have been on the course was 90 years of age.

The signal box outside of Kingsmere Station was purpose built for the site but all the equipment within it comes from old redundant signal boxes. The signalling system is mainly of the traffic light kind,

Minimum age of participants is 10 years. Minimum height 1.4m (4ft 7 ins). Maximum weight 20.5 stones (130kg). Under 18 yr olds must be accompanied by a participating adult. The assault course operates in all weathers, other than in icy or stormy conditions or during lightning. The Go Ape cabin is a few minutes walk from the car park.

Go Ape, Moors Valley Country Park, Horton Road, Ashley Heath, Ringwood, Hants, BH24 2ET. Open March to October 0900 – 1700. Prior booking essential (Tel: 0845 643 9132).

There are now 17 steam and 2 diesel locomotives all of which have been designed and made on site, with the exception of the originals brought from Christchurch. The driver sits within the engine cab. The trains are all 46 inches high, 26 inches wide and have a length up to 17 feet. Each weighs approximately one ton. In addition to the engines, there are 36 passenger vehicles. Typically a train consists of an engine, pulling 12 carriages with seating for 72 passengers. On some days only a single train may be operating, whereas on others there can be as many as 15.

although semaphore signals are in operation in the station area. Telephones are located around the track in case an engine driver needs to communicate with the signal box in an emergency.

For Lakeside Station follow the sign to the information centre and the station is to the left of the centre. If Lakeside Station is closed then Kingsmere Station is ¼ mile along the path that runs alongside the track.

The railway is open everyday from May to September. It opens at other times of the year, especially at weekends and school holidays and it is best to check beforehand. Trains run from 1045 to 1700. Tel: 01425 471415.

There are no admission charges to enter Moors Park but there are car-parking charges. Open from 0800 – dusk.

Take the A338 Ringwood Road out of Bournemouth. At the main roundabout, six miles beyond the speed derestriction sign go straight ahead (second exit). The entrance to the Park is 1½ miles along the road on the right.

No. 36 Wilts & Dorset bus stops at the entrance to the park.

CHALLENGE LEISURE

Challenge Leisure offers you an opportunity to take part in some unusual but interesting sports, namely paintballing, clay pigeon shooting, quadbiking and archery. The centre is one of the few UK Paintball Sports Federation accredited venues in Dorset and paintballing is one of the fastest growing sports in the country. Two teams start at opposite ends of the field and attempt to achieve their objective. The course can take in both open ground and woodland. Their 'guns' shoot paintballs that contain a colour dye which marks the opponent on impact. This either eliminates that opponent from the game or the number of hits are taken into account at the end of the game. Players are provided with protective goggles, overalls and a 'gun'. The activity is suitable for all ages. There are minimum and maximum numbers for each activity but if you are on your own or in a small group then the centre will try to include you with other groups. There are minimum ages for the various activities. And full instructions are given in each sport.

Challenge Leisure, Wigbeth Farm, Horton Road, Horton, Dorset BH21 7JH. Tel: Ralph 07768 305666.
Open all year but phone to reserve a session. (01202 877899) Prices vary with activity and time spent.

Follow the directions to the Moors Valley Country Park. Continue past the park and after 4¼ miles is Tree Tops and the entrance to Challenge Leisure. Go through the gate and drive slowly down the track road for 400 yards.

RINGWOOD TOWN AND COUNTRY EXPERIENCE

This 30,000 square feet of exhibition space traces the history of Ringwood over the years. The museum was started four years ago using the owner's private collection. There are a number of Stone- and Bronze-Age arrow heads excavated within 100 yards of the museum. Smuggling was a way of life in the area at the end of the 17th century and there is a display of the tools used and where the smugglers were trading. The exhibits include a full size replica of Ringwood railway platform as it was 80 years ago, old shops, vintage vehicles and a Bouncing Bomb. The bomb would have been

dropped by a Lancaster Bomber and was found in pieces in a field. It has been carefully restored and would have weighed 9 tons when full of explosives. The latest exhibit is the cockpit of a Hawker Hunter Jet. The Cunarder is a model roundabout made by Les Dorland who was a Senior Engineer on the Queen Mary. It is made totally of metal taken from the ship and took him 30 years to build. He died just before it was completed. The museum is interactive even to the extent of inviting visitors to try on some of the clothes such as the old army uniforms. The museum has a large archive of material, including records of Ringwood going back more than 200 years.

Ringwood Town and Country Experience, Salisbury Road, Blashford, Ringwood, Hampshire, BH24 3PA Tel: 01425 472746. Daily 1000 – 1630 throughout the year but closed on Saturdays from November – Easter. Coffee shop and restaurant.

Take the A338 Ringwood Road out of Bournemouth. At the main roundabout, six miles beyond the speed derestriction sign, turn right (third exit) onto the A31. 1 mile further on take the left fork (B3347) signposted to Ringwood. Turn left at the roundabout (first exit) and the Town and Country Experience is ½ mile on the left.

RINGWOOD BREWERY

The Ringwood Brewery opened in 1978 on a site that had previously been that of a brewery dating back to 1760; immediately prior to Ringwood Brewery taking it over the site was a derelict engineers yard. The brewery expanded to its present location in 1986. In 2007 the brewery became part of the Marston Group, employing over 50 staff and producing 34,000 barrels of top quality real ale a year, or about 11 million pints!

rapidly becomes noisy as the beer is steadily sampled! The brewery owns a number of local pubs including The Inn on the Furlong in Ringwood.

On a visit to the brewery, visitors are offered an initial drink in the brewery's pub and then taken on a 30 minute tour of the brewery where the brewing process is explained. The brewing process takes about seven days – one day to brew, three or four for it to ferment and another three or four for the beer to mature. At the end of the tour the group returns to the pub where several of the brewery's nine beers are sampled. What may have started out as a quiet tour

Ringwood Brewery, 138 Christchurch Road, Ringwood, Hampshire, BH24 3AP. Tel: 01425 470303 or 01425 471177. Saturday tours at 1200, 1400 and 1600 all year, other than December. There is a souvenir half-pint glass and the sampling of beers. Children under 8 not allowed and 8 – 17 year olds must be accompanied by an adult.

Take the A338 Ringwood Road out of Bournemouth. At the main roundabout, 6 miles beyond the speed derestriction sign, turn right (third exit) onto the A31. 1 mile further on take the left fork (B3347) signposted to Ringwood. Turn right at the roundabout (third exit). Keep on the B3347 across the next roundabout, left at the next mini-roundabout and across the next roundabout. The brewery is on the right.

If travelling from the Town and Country Experience then return to the roundabout and carry straight on (second exit) and follow the B3347 as above.

MILLSTREAM MODEL RACEWAY

Millstream is the UK's leading slot car centre. The British Slot Car Club was formed in 1997 in Westbourne and moved to its present site a year later and developed the centre to its present form. There are currently two tracks on display, both are custom made and produced by the world leading Ogilvie manufacturer. The 210 ft track, with eight lanes, is the largest in the UK. The second track is 140 ft long, also has eight lanes and can accommodate models on a scale of 1:24. There are also radio controlled cars, model railways and a shop selling a wide range of model equipment.

Millstream Model Raceway, 11 Millstream Trading Estate, Christchurch Road, Ringwood, Hampshire BH24 3SB. 01425 489939. Open: Tuesday – Saturday 1000 – 1700. Closed Mondays.

Follow the directions to the Ringwood Brewery; the entrance to the Millstream Trading Estate is another 200 yards on the right and the Raceway is 200 yards into the trading estate on the left.

LIBERTY'S RAPTOR AND REPTILE CENTRE

The centre is home to a large collection of raptors. i.e. birds of prey, in particular eagles, owls and vultures. In addition there are common reptiles such as snakes, lizards and tortoises. The centre used to be run by a charity but it closed and was taken over by the present owners in 2003 and opened to the public in 2005. There is a rescue centre that takes in injured birds of prey and later releases them back into the wild. The birds are often taken to local schools to give children first hand knowledge of them. The centre is named after it's American Bald Eagle, 'Liberty'. She was born in Kent in 1999.

There are 20 different species of reptiles.

Throughout the day there are displays when birds can be seen flying freely. In all there are 130 birds of prey and an impressive 22 species of owls. Most of the birds can be seen at close quarters. It is possible to touch the birds during the flying displays and look them straight in the eye. However make sure you do not stroke them from behind as they are likely to think you are attacking!

Falconry was practised in the New Forest for centuries and it was here that King William II was killed in August 1100 when a stray arrow hit him in the eye. For those wishing to learn the skill of falconry, courses are held in the nearby New Forest. Participants must be at least 16 years of age. Experience of handling and flying the hawks, owls and vultures is offered for those over 10 years. There are also photo days

There is a small café and an indoor display area in the event of bad weather.

Crow Lane, Crow, Nr Ringwood, Hampshire BH24 3EA, Tel: 01425 476487. Open: Daily March to October 1000 – 1700 and weekends only from November to February 1000 – 1600.

Follow the directions to Millstream Model Raceway and continue on for a further ½ mile. Turn left at the Texaco garage and continue for another ½ mile. Turn left at the crossroads and Liberty's Raptor and Reptile Centre is 200 yards on the left.